David Adamovich, Joachim Heil
&
Lady Astrid

A DAY ON BROADWAY

THE ART OF BEING
A KNIFE THROWER'S ASSISTANT

==
Turnshare Ltd.
London

published by

Turnshare Ltd.
27, Old Gloucester Street
London WC1N 3XX

E-mail: publisher@turnshare.com
homepage:
http:/www.turnshare.com

Copyright © 2005 by Turnshare Ltd.
All rights reserved

Made and printed by
Turnshare Ltd., London

ISBN 1-903343-73-9

A Day on Broadway ...

is dedicated to all target girls – past, present and future – out of respect, admiration and gratitude for taking all the risks and, at the same time, making their knife throwing partner look so good!

"For, to speak out once for all, man only plays when in the full meaning of the word he is a man, and he is only completely a man when he plays."

Friedrich Schiller

Preface

A DAY ON BROADWAY is based on the true-life recollections of a significant day in the life of three people. That day was Monday, August 5, 2002.

It is about The Great Throwdini (The Rev. Dr. David Adamovich), a retired professor, minister and professional knife thrower from New York, Dr. Joachim Heil, a doctor of philosophy with a love for dangerous circus acts from Mainz, Germany and Lady Astrid (Astrid Schollenberger), Joachim's unsuspecting girlfriend destined to become the knife thrower's assistant.

In a nutshell, they came together to perform a live knife throwing performance (the impalement arts) at New York's longest running magic show, Monday Night Magic, playing at the McGinn/Cazale Theatre on Broadway and 76th Street in NYC.

This was Throwdini's first appearance at Monday Night Magic — something he had been working on for nearly two years. It was Joachim's master plan to bring Throwdini to Germany to perform for a group from Mainz University AND to introduce his girlfriend, Astrid, to Throwdini with the hope he would use her as his assistant. Did Astrid know what Joachim was planning? Anyway, they all got what they wanted. Everybody's dreams came true and THIS IS what happened.

Foreword

A BRIEF HISTORY OF KNIFE THROWING — Then and Now

Skill, sex, danger – three ingredients which the showman uses, not necessarily in that order, to draw a crowd and provide a show which entertains by thrilling the audience. The knife throwing act is the classic example, in both fact and fiction, allowing the spectator to wonder at the skill and daring of the performers while giving the frisson of excitement in the face of danger.

Make no mistake, a golden rule for the thrower: that is real steel thudding into the board, only millimetres from unflinching flesh. Both performers are as fully aware as the spectator of the consequences of a mistake. There are no special effects, no hidden knives to spring out of the board, no chance of a replay. This is live entertainment. What you see is happening before you, even if you view with covered eyes while peeping between closed fingers.

What the audience sees is the results of hours of dedicated practice to hone the thrower's skill until it becomes second nature and careful preparation by the performers to balance the risks of any stunt against their desire to present the most thrilling experience.

Knife throwing performers appeared in Europe in the 19th century at country fairs and travelling shows. During the second half of the century, the increasing urbanization due to industrialization produced the conditions for a more prosperous populace and shows became a major element in fairground entertainment. In an age before cinema, or today's mass media, these shows provided exciting live entertainment. Performers were "gypsies" or an occasional Chinese troupe. In 1887 Buffalo Bill brought his Congress of Riders to

Europe, giving a command performance before Queen Victoria in the UK and returned to Europe with the show two years later. This resulted in a wave of popularity for the Wild West Show and the western skills of the lasso and sharp shooting. Knife throwing, which was not originally performed in the American shows, was now introduced into the "Western Pastimes" and became a major component of acts, usually presented as a "cowboy" or "Red Indian," performing both in travelling shows, and also in the emergent variety theatres in large towns. Knife throwing was often combined with sharp shooting by rifle, or bow and arrow, and also whip and rope skills. In the US, these acts were found in midway shows on fairgrounds and also in rodeo and touring Western shows.

The introduction of the cinema and later of television sounded the death knell for much of the traditional live entertainment during the second half of the twentieth century, taking with it vaudeville, variety, and the midway show. However, the circus, especially in the UK and Europe, with many smaller shows still surviving, has continued to provide a place for the "Western act." Today there seems to be some revival in the public's appetite for live entertainment, be it in smaller outdoor fairs, mall shows, or the more intimate style of cabaret. Knife throwing artistes working so close to their audience, accentuate the thrill and excitement of their dangerous performances.

The basic elements of the "Impalement Act" are the thrower, a variety of weapons, including knives, axes, spears, machetes, a large wooden target board, and most importantly, an attractive assistant for a living "target." In its simplest form the act consists of the girl posing provocatively in various positions in front of the board to be outlined by the blades. And even in this simple form the spectator is intensely aware of the skill, trust, co-ordination and sheer nerve required by both participants of the act. Those blades are thrown with sufficient force to deeply pierce the wood. The sound of the impact heightens the realization of the consequences of even the slightest error in aim. The thrower aims his blade mere inches from his assistant's unprotected flesh, but just a minor error can produce a hit drastically close to his trusting assistant — a hit so close they each know immediately as it puts an unobservable and brief shiver down both their spines.

Successive artistes have developed the basic routine with stunts of greater difficulty for the thrower and consequent risk for his partner. Throwers work with a blindfold or throw the blades through a paper screen which covers their hidden assistant. The basic throwing knife will weigh nearly 1 pound, but the other types of "ammunition" used include fire knives, axes and tomahawks, swords and spears.

In the 1930s several European artistes made the decisive development of having a moving target, by strapping their partner to a spinning wheel, "The Wheel of Death". In 1938, the Gibsons, coming from Germany, introduced the Wheel into the US and, a year later, chilled the blood of the New York circus audience by hiding the girl with a paper screen covering the spinning wheel. This is a stunt that severely stretches the boundaries for a consistently safe performance and very few artistes have subsequently attempted it. At about this time, a Hungarian couple added their own version of difficulty when Collins balanced on one foot on a tightrope to throw his knives around Elizabeth spinning on the wheel, a feat later repeated by a Swiss duo, the Tornados. Since its initial introduction, The Wheel has become a feature of many acts but never fails to raise gasps from the audience. One circus troupe even found room to strap two girls, head to toe, on the same wheel.

Other variations on a moving target include the "Devil's Door" rotating on a vertical axis. This has been regularly shown by Larry Cisewski in the US. The great German family, The Brumbachs, evolved a complicated variation with a revolving target "door" having a center section which spins horizontally on a centre axis, allowing Fritz to throw his knives around his wife Helga and daughter Sylvia as they spin rapidly, head over heels, on opposite sides of the door. Fritz Brumbach is widely regarded as one of the greatest knife throwing artistes and over his career continually extended the scope of the knife throwing act. He is notable for throwing heavy axes around his partner/wife Helga from a huge distance of 40 feet away – blindfolded! On retirement, his son Patrick continues the tradition of introducing new and exciting presentations.

There have been a few woman throwers in the professional scene, working both with men and women standing at the board and one couple in the UK regularly exchange places during their routine, but even in an age of women's liberation, the traditional arrangement of male thrower and female partner still prevails.

The Great Throwdini, a.k.a. The Rev. Dr. David Adamovich, is not only an unusual addition to the ranks of international artistes, but has developed an act suitable for the times. He took up knife throwing and entered the professional scene in his mid mid-fifties despite no previous experience in show business. But to prove that age is no barrier to success, he became a world champion competition thrower and has now developed his own uniquely styled cabaret, stage and circus act, appropriately titled MAXIMUM RISK. No false cowboy, he appears in immaculate evening dress in a presentation ideally suited to the more intimate venues where he is fully able to interact with the members of his audience. Noted for the speed of his throwing, his routines include the most testing stunts combined with charm and humour.

Combining an exhibition of skill and co-ordination with the erotic appeal of a beautiful woman submitting to extreme danger, the knife throwing act continues to present an exciting spectacle which can cause that intake of breath and a tingle in the spine of the audience. We relate to the display of nerve and courage by that "target girl," but do not realize the nerve needed by the thrower as he maintains the concentration required to ensure the essential safety of his partner. A Day on Broadway delves into the minds of both The Great Throwdini and his assistant, The Lovely and Daring Lady Astrid. Take a deep-breath, tightly grasp the arm rests of your chair and sit back, for in just a moment you'll soon be on the edge of your seat as you experience the inner thoughts of the thrower and his partner.

Stanley Brion, London, February 2005

Table of Contents

Preface — v

Foreword — vii
A BRIEF HISTORY OF
KNIFE THROWING — Then and Now
by Stanley Brion, London

Introduction — xv
by Simon Lovell, New York

A Day On Broadway — 1
from The Great Throwdini's point of view

A Day On Broadway — 29
The Art of being a knife thrower's assistant
from Lady Astrid's point of view

A Short Philosophical Essay — 83
on the Art of Knife Throwing
by Joachim Heil, Ph.D.

Autobiographical notes about — 121
The Great Throwdini

Fellow Performers — 159
Who've Influenced Throwdini

A Treatise on the Art and Science — 171
of Throwing Knives
by Dr. David Adamovich
THE GREAT THROWDINI

Introduction

I had just arrived at the McGinn/Cazale Theatre in NYC and was starting to prepare my props for my headline performance that evening for Monday Night Magic, NYC's longest ever running magic and comedy show, when the producer, Michael Chaut, informed me the that middle act was a knife thrower. This was great news! As a young man I had worked with a traveling fair (Americans read that as Carnival!) and had both seen and was a total fan of the, so-called, 10 in 1 acts that worked the midway in tent shows. For just a dollar, "Roll up, roll up my friends!" one could witness fire-eaters, sword-swallowers, geeks, fat and/or bearded ladies, electric girls, escape artistes and, of course, the occasional knife thrower! With the demise of such shows it is incredibly rare these days to catch any one of these eccentric folk performing at all. Knife throwers are among the rarest of all. I was a happy camper indeed!

With some extensive detective work (ok, I read the program) I discovered that the 'thrower' for this evening was called THE GREAT THROWDINI and was purported to be a world champion of his art. Raising my curiosity level even more was finding out his German partner, THE LOVELY AND DARING LADY ASTRID, had flown to NYC just three days prior. Cool, some wild west knife throwing sounded like fun. All the knife throwers I had seen wore native American Indian gear so I had always perceived the genre to be a wild west type act, hence my thinking on what I was soon to see. I was wrong of course but Throwdini is a "one-of" as you'll soon discover!

Like many performers I rarely watch the acts that are on before me. If they are awful it puts me down, if they are wonderful it can instill fear that I've got to follow them. Sometimes it's just best not to know! That night, however, I got a good seat for Throwdini and sat back to enjoy.

And enjoy I did. Throwdini, or Throw as I call him these days, dressed in a tux and hand tied bow tie (no wild west influence here!) did some incredible stuff. Not just knifes but axes, machetes and more were hurled through the air around the young lady partnering him. Their execution, timing and interaction were perfect. It appeared as though they had been performing together for years; he threw and she seduced the audience with her courage and charm. It was a rare treat to witness their performance. He threw blindfolded! Damn it, he even threw through an opaque sheet of paper that the lady held up in front of herself and didn't hit her once. And then, if that were not enough, we then witnessed his lovely partner spinning on The Wheel of Death as he hurled knives on both sides of her body. When The Wheel stopped spinning she threw her arm up in the air and in her lovely accent triumphantly exclaimed, "Throwdini." Like everybody else in the audience I was on the edge of my seat and, at the end, we all breathed a collective sigh of relief that the lady was unharmed and the knife thrower had won. The applause was both loud and long. This was a class act in every sense of the word!

I made it my job to meet this extraordinary man and we have since become very good friends indeed. This pool hall owning, gourmet chef, minister, highly educated, knife and other assorted sharp objects throwing kind of guy is never boring. He's a delight to be around. He's a great friend to have not to mention a great act to watch!

The only time I haven't enjoyed it quite so much was when Throw convinced me to dress up as a lady (a very long story) and stand in for his partner (an even longer story) who was unavailable. If you think it's frightening watching a knife thrower, then try standing against the board. I had various stains in my panties midway through the performance! It did, however, give me a somewhat unique insight into the extraordinary talent, precision and confidence that makes the difference between the mediocre and the great. I thought the knives looked close to the girl before, but when one of them actually sliced through the cloth of the dress I was wearing, close didn't seem an appropriate expression. My actual expression is unprintable here but, trust me, Throw doesn't mess about, those knives are really close!

I'm delighted that some of his amusements and amazements are chronicled here in these pages. While nothing can prepare you for the real experience that is Throw, it might give you a bit of an idea.

These days I occasionally emcee Monday Night Magic and am always thrilled when Throw is on the bill. The first time I introduced him the words sprang forth without a thought. The introduction has remained the same ever since. Enjoy these pages as I give you, "The man, the myth, the legend, the talent that is…The Great Throwdini!"

Enjoy!

>Simon Lovell, New York, Feb 2005
>Star of the hit Off-Broadway show, STRANGE AND UNUSUAL HOBBIES

A Day On Broadway
from The Great Throwdini's point of view

Authoring this memoir of an event that occurred over two years ago brings back such wonderful memories. As a writer, two comments come to mind: a) my uncle Ray once said, "Don't let the truth get in the way of a good story," and b) Garrison Keillor, a well known radio host claimed that every great story should have four elements: sex, money, religion and mystery.

Therefore, beginning a story with, "The banker's daughter exclaimed, 'Oh my God, I'm pregnant and I don't know who did it,'" would be pretty cool. But, in response to Uncle Ray, every-thing you're about to read is the truth, the whole truth and nothing but the truth. In meeting Keillor's requirements I'd say he has no idea of what it's like being in the shoes of an impalement artist. Sex, money, religion and mystery don't even scratch the surface of where this story is going. After all, I throw "real knives, machetes, axes at a beautiful, scantily clad woman on stage for a living. What could be better than that?" (This was the line Michael Chaut, founder and co-producer of Monday Night

Magic, used when introducing me to The Discovery Channel's special, Magic Road Trip, shot during one of our performances at the McGinn/Cazale Theater on Broadway.)

How it all began ... I was only performing as a professional knife thrower for about one year. My assistant and I had made arrangements with Joachim Heil to perform for a group from Mainz University, Germany. We packed our costumes, knives and accessories and headed for Germany. We were met at the airport by Joachim and his girlfriend, Astrid Schollenberger. Plans were made to perform. Everything was "under control." I had, at Joachim's request, modified one stunt to include Astrid. Little did I know what affect that would have.

My assistant and I were speeding along the Autobahn toward Mainz from Bamberg after visiting my daughter Tracy, a West Point graduate and now officer, serving in the US Army. I explained the modified routine to my assistant who, much to my surprise, got rather angry stating the stunt I was going to use Astrid for was "HER" stunt and no one else was allowed to do it. Well that didn't go over very well with me, Joachim or Astrid. The bottom line was, I had made a promise to Joachim and Astrid and I was going to keep it despite my assistant's objections.

Astrid was excellent and showed only the slightest fear of the knives at first. I noticed she was flinching as the knife hit the board. Joachim and I filmed her up close and pointed this out. To me it was outrageously obvious. Then again, I was looking for it. After she understood what she was doing, I asked her to look right into my eyes and to flirt with me in a way only a woman could do (with Joachim's approval, of course). She did. I looked back at her and even made eye contact as I was throwing. An experienced professional thrower doesn't have to look at the precise spot where the knife is thrown. It's in his "mind's eye." (For that matter, there

are two "blind" stunts in the routine in which I am either blindfolded or cannot see my assistant as she is hidden behind a paper veil. "Seeing" the spot where the knife goes is purely academic.)

So the time came for the show. Astrid was psyched. I was psyched. The moment for her first stunt was there. We did it perfectly. Just one thing got in the way. One bloody little event that proved she was a pro. When it was all over and I asked her how she continued she simply said, "The show must go on." Here's what happened. As I turn to prepare knives for the next stunt and have a talk with the audience, my assistant pulls the knives from the board and puts them back in my case. Astrid had difficulty with one that was stuck pretty deep into the wood. Instead of pushing it up and down and pulling backward she decided to wedge her finger under the knife to create a lever effect. That was definitely the wrong thing to do. The edge cut right into her finger right down to the bone. I turned from my box and saw her standing there with blood running down the board. As I ran over to see what happened she was already reaching for a cloth to wrap around her finger. She simply looked at me and said, "Let's go. I'm ready for the next stunt." Now that's a pro. I knew right then and there she was the one to assist me in my upcoming Monday Night Magic performance.

Before leaving for Germany I told Joachim and Astrid about the upcoming booking I had in three months; it would be my first appearance at Monday Night Magic, then in it's fifth year. After Astrid's performance in Mainz, there was little doubt I wanted to use her and mentioned this to them realizing how wild and crazy the idea was. After all, this was for all intents and purposes THE BIG TIME and I'd be using a new, inexperienced assistant. Only two or three non-magician variety acts get to perform at Monday Night Magic which is, after all, a magic show; and that's what the paying audience is coming to see. The variety acts that do perform there

usually add at least one magic trick so as not to disappoint the audience. To this day I still have people insisting that my entire act is magic, i.e., the knives come from the back of the board. THEY DON'T — I REALLY THROW THEM. Thank you, it's the truth.

As fate would have it the assistant who came with me to Germany and I were booked to perform in an off-off Broadway play, Big Top, in which she had a talking part as the knife thrower's assistant and I was her husband who threw knives around her as she performed her lines. Not approaching that gig as an actor I didn't care about not getting a talking part. I got something even better, I was cast as Throwdini — in essence I had the opportunity of playing myself! The play was for a six week run two shows per week. By the second week things had gotten so bad between my assistant (remember, the one I took to Germany) and me, that I was forced to either pull out or have a serious talk with the producer about her behavior. One case in point, I would normally take her hands and back her into position at the board. I put my hands up for her to take and she just backed away from me leaving me standing there literally empty handed. It was sorely obvious to the audience. After the show she explained, "You missed your cue." Bottom line, I agreed to stay for the sake of the play but the tension was so thick "you could have cut it with a knife." I advertised in a well-known show business paper for a knife thrower's assistant and several girls applied.

Two actually showed up under cover to watch the play and to speak with me afterward expressing their interest in the job. I selected the one with show business experience and it turned out to be a good choice. She was very attractive and added a nice touch to the act. I explained to her, however, that even though Monday Night Magic was coming up in two months that I had made a commitment to Astrid. She accepted the job and also understood my promise to Astrid.

Astrid and Joachim arrived in America. I picked them up at JFK International and could only imagine what was going on in their heads. After all, they flew across the Atlantic for Astrid to be my assistant for what amounted to 18 minutes of glory. I knew, he knew, and she knew it was all about one thing — we were going to end the show with The Wheel of Death. The finale of finales. The piece de resistance. The Wheel of Death. What's in a name? "That which we call a rose. By any other name would smell as sweet." Shakespeare. The Wheel of What? Why, the Wheel of Death. What else? Also known as LA RUEDA DE LA MUERTE (Spanish), DAS RAD DES TODES (German), LA ROUE DE LA MORT (French), HET WIEL VAN DOOD (Dutch), LA ROTELLA DELLA MORTE (Italian), and A RODA DA MORTE (Portuguese).

Yes, it is the one thing most associated with the professional knife thrower. It's the one thing that comes up more than anything else in every conversation about knife throwing. You either do it or you don't. You are either a knife thrower or you're not. Once again, I knew, he knew, and she knew it was the FIRST time I would be performing The Wheel on stage. Hours and hours. Hundreds, perhaps thousands of knives went into many practice boards using a mannequin to perfect the timing. After all, the difference between success and a serious oops was whittled down to hundredths of a second. There are two ways to do The Wheel: one knife per revolution OR two knives per revolution. One famous thrower, Paul LaCross, was known for his one knife per revolution. Although his wheel rotated pretty fast it's just not the same as doing the stunt with two knives per revolution, i.e., one knife on each side of the girl for each revolution; one when the head is up and one when the head is down. The timing is very critical. For the most part the stunt is done at between 1.2 and 1.4 seconds per revolution. This results in knives thrown at a frequency of 0.6 to 0.7 seconds/throw.

Considering the time from hand to board is approximately 0.2 seconds means the ability and decision to grab the next knife, pull it back and then to throw it at an open piece of board as it whizzes by occurs in about one-half second — the proverbial split second, over and over, until the hand full of knives is empty. Most throwers use between eight and twelve knives. The stunt is essentially over within eight seconds from when the thrower steps back to throw and he's stepping in to stop the wheel's rotation.

So now Joachim and Astrid are here. Two days before the show. We had just two days to practice the entire routine and to rehearse The Wheel. Under the critical eye of Joachim, my wife Barbara, and other family that came by to see what we were up to, we rehearsed the show over and over. Perhaps 80 knives, axes, tomahawks and machetes were thrown during each set. Each step, bow and pause was choreographed and evaluated. Even my lines were down pat. After all, it's a show. It's a rehearsed show with no surprises to the performers. Astrid quickly learned the reason for each different set of knives in my box. Unlike other performers who use the same knives over and over for each profile/stunt, I use about five different sets. Each set has a specific purpose as the audience can see the difference between twelve and sixteen inch knives as they are thrown. It adds to the mystique and drama of the performance. This was stated so well in the Scorcese movie Gangs of New York as the audience called for a "Command performance...an exciting exhibition of skill, courage, daring and drama…the Wheel of Death." No truer words could be spoken. This is what we were rehearsing for. The McGinn/Cazale Theatre at 76th on Broadway was about to get a real performance of the impalement arts leading to The Wheel of Death. They were about to see a knife thrower formally dressed in tails, red bow tie and cummerbund throw knives at a "scantily clad female" strapped to The Wheel of Death. We were excited and rightfully so.

We rehearsed, rehearsed and rehearsed over and over for two days in typically hot and humid late summer days on the waterfront in Freeport, NY. Those passing on boats in the canal were amused. Some would even stop and literally drop anchor. On occasion we'd

even get applause. But our minds were not on that audience; it was the upcoming show at Monday Night Magic in a couple of days that weighed heavily upon us. Astrid dressed in her leotard costume. I rehearsed in a circus type of shirt rather than tails. It was too hot to get my tuxedo soaked in sweat. I suppose there were about 80 knives, axes, and hawks total in the entire show. It was a lot of hardware and steel to be tossing around in a relatively short period of time. We'd set everything up, queue the music and begin. Each time we made a mistake in either our lines or our steps we'd review the mistake and redo the entire stunt. Unlike a circus act in which we would both quickly retrieve the knives from the board, my cabaret style act for Monday Night Magic allows me to interact with the audience while my assistant pulls the knives. This makes it much easier for me, the thrower, and also allows me the opportunity to mockingly scold people in the front few rows for admiring my assistant instead of listening me while I'm doing my lines. As Gabor tells his assistant Adele in the French movie Girl on The Bridge, "It's not the thrower that counts, it's the target." No truer words could be said regarding the audience's attention during a show. Thus, we work this type of interaction even into the rehearsal. Over and over I would invite Astrid to look at and flirt with someone who was watching our rehearsals as well as with me. I wanted her to get used to interacting with the audience. She is not a piece of meat standing at the board. To the audience she may appear to be in danger. The reality is that she's put her trust in my skill as a knife thrower, and artist who has learned to miss — as well as hit — whatever he aims at, depending on the situation. She is the proverbial damsel in distress yet totally safe in the hands of her thrower.

 The day of the show was upon us, as though it were a relief of some kind. Two days of rehearsals with at least times on The Wheel. It's worth mentioning that with each spin on The Wheel there was

always the lingering doubt in the back of my mind that Astrid was getting sick. After all, it's an unusual experience to spin head over heels in a circular motion around your abdomen looking at someone with a hand full of knives looking back at you! It's definitely worth mentioning here, if not one hundred times more, that I have the utmost respect and admiration for my assistants. Just standing at the board is a feat unto itself. The knives come speeding in at about 30 mph, at less than one second apart and suddenly thud into the wood just inches from flesh. In fact there are times when the knife comes to rest against the assistant's body. Such an event is common whenever the knives are thrown above, versus to the side of, a body part. This was something I had to warn Astrid about. Moreover I had to explain that she should not be startled or to think she was hit. Yes, to some degree the spinning knife can make contact but it's actually along the edge in contrast to the point. Getting hit with the point is something we don't even consider and is the basis for the trust between thrower and assistant. If she doubts my ability to throw or I lack confidence in her ability to remain still or not look scared, we have a big problem. This is something I always look for when "breaking-in" a new assistant. Even the slightest flinch is not good. She must overcome that immediately or we've got no place to go.

We were off to Manhattan from Long Island, just 30 miles or about a one hour drive. Every one in the car was silent. Perhaps my wife was the most excited. She was in the middle of it all. Every aspect of the past few days was lived by her as much as us. She heard me over and over expressing my fears and anxieties over The Wheel. We were met at the theater by those who were assisting in the load-in and set-up. Harry (Der Werfer) Munroe and Joe Torraca. Harry was the first real knife thrower I ever met. He taught me how to throw a one half spin. Today he makes my knives; Throwdini Throwers by Der Werfer. Joe introduced me to knife throwing about five years prior to Monday Night Magic. He too wanted to be there for our debut. Board after board, loads of hardware, costumes and boxes of knives and axes were brought up to the third floor where Monday Night Magic performs at the McGinn/Cazale Theatre, atop

the Promenade theatre on the ground floor. It's an interesting place to perform in. The audience actually sits in ascending seats that go from the third to the fourth floor. Somewhere in that dark place beyond the lights would soon be a couple hundred people waiting to be entertained. Little did they know they'd see a knife thrower on the bill as they expected three magic acts.

So we all hauled everything up onto the stage, assembled the flat board and The Wheel, set up the tables to hold our knives, her balloons, the champagne bucket filled with axes, tomahawks, etc. Then we had to push it all off to the side to allow room for the first act. It was at least an hour before show time and only 30 minutes before the audience would be allowed into the theatre. Off we went to the dressing rooms. Make-up, costumes, my bow-tie had to be tied and on and on. So many things to take care of while the opening act took stage. Unknown to Astrid I asked Der Werfer to sneak off to a florist and purchase a dozen roses that I wanted to present to

her as a surprise as she stepped through the paper veil. He told me afterward it might not have happened. The first florist he went into wanted about $50. He walked out and knew he could do better; he was not the kind of guy to be had. Apparently he found another store along Broadway that sold them at a reasonable cost. I offered to pay but he refused. They were perfect and the look on her face was priceless.

And there we were, standing behind the curtain listening to the announcer, Jamy Ian Swiss (a coproducer of Monday Night Magic) make the introduction. He found a pretty cool way to introduce a variety act into a magic venue,

"Our next act may not be magic but what he does is quite magical. Please welcome World Champion Knife Thrower, The Great Throwdini and his assistant Lady Astrid."

Our pulses were pounding as we ran out on stage, arm in arm, me with a hand full of knives and each of us taking our place on stage for the first stunt. The routine was quite basic for me. It starts with one impalement type stunt and then goes into some target style throwing into balloons and a pie plate. Astrid then brings an audience member up on stage and we scare him with a hood

over his head as we pretend to pop balloons from under his arms and between his legs.

I threw axes into the board as Astrid broke the balloons with a pin. We then go into a series of classic impalement art profiles that included: throwing knives rapidly up one side of her body followed by a very tight profile up the front of her as she turns and backs up against the first set; throwing two sets of knives that I retrieve from my pockets using both the left and right hand; throwing a set of knives outlining her body as she arches backward exposing her throat; throwing large knives, axes, tomahawks and machetes to

either side of her; a double blind stunt in which I wear a mask and hood and throw to the sound of her tapping loudly on the board; throwing six axes along the sides of her body as she stands hidden behind a six by four foot veil of butcher paper; and ultimately The Wheel of Death.

Honestly speaking The Wheel loomed over my head in a way that can barely be described. Let's try this. The applause from the last stunt is over. You're about to introduce the next stunt to the audience with a small description. "Ladies and Gentlemen, The Wheel of Death. The one thing most associated in everyone's mind when they envision knife throwing. It was introduced to America in 1938 by the Gibsons. We know it as The Wheel of Death. Astrid calls it Das Rad." I turned to Astrid, put up my hands for her to take and said,

"Astrid, Das Rad." At that point I led her across stage, helped her up on the foot pedal, strapped her in at the waist, picked up a hand full of knives, started spinning The Wheel, stepped back and grabbed that first knife.

But wait. Stop the clock. Those little doubting demons start banging around in your head. What's it like? Assume you're dreadfully fearful of heights. You suddenly find yourself at the door of a plane with a parachute strapped to your back. It's your turn to jump. It's a defining moment in your life. You jump or you don't. You decide at that moment what you're made of. That's the only way to describe what it's like standing there, for the very first time, in public, in front of a theatre full of people, The Wheel spinning with a girl strapped to it,

and you're holding a hand full of knives dressed in a tailed tuxedo. Can you imagine? It's not only a do or die moment for the assistant. It's a do or die moment for the thrower. OK, start the clock. Grab, throw, grab, throw, grab, throw, etc. until all the knives are gone. She did her part. I did mine. I ran in to stop The Wheel from spinning. Astrid threw her left hand up into the air and yelled, "Throwdini."

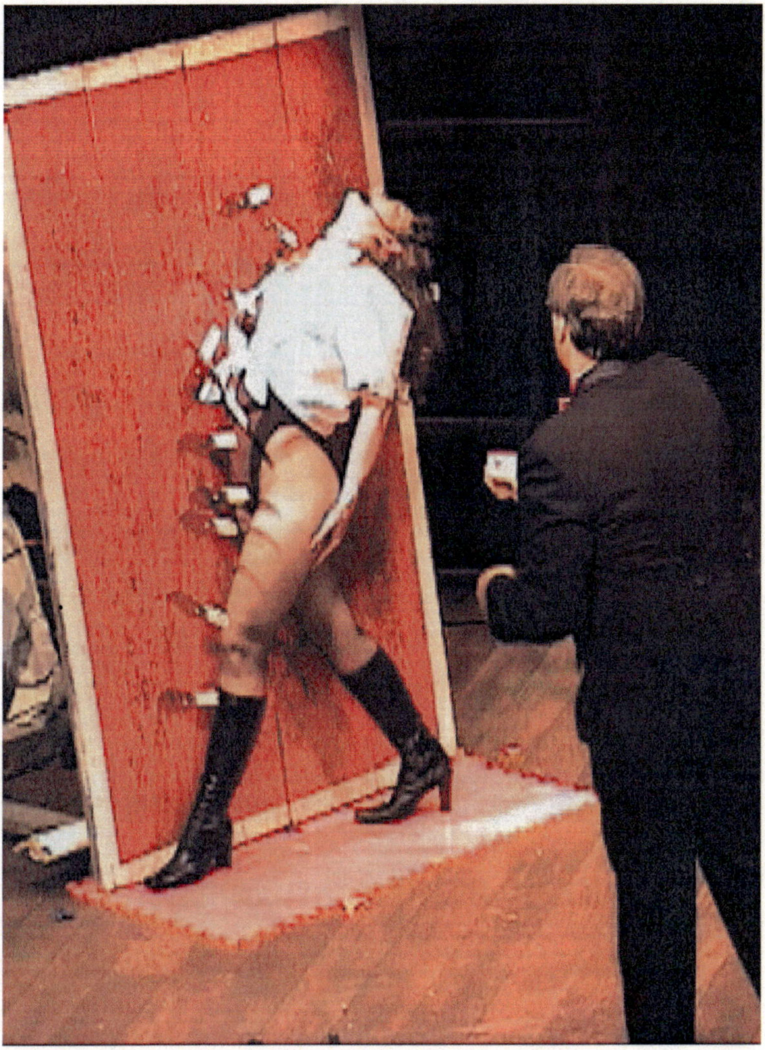

It immediately prompted a standing ovation. The standing "O" to The Wheel was one of the finest moments in my life. It was over. We did it and as any pilot would tell you, "Any landing you walk away from is a good one." We walked off that stage and felt like we just landed the Concorde on its maiden flight. The whole world was

watching and cheering. But what about the rest of the routine? There were such wonderful moments to reflect upon.

A few stand out among the others. For the opening stunt Astrid was wearing a wrap around type of skirt over her leotard. In my usual fashion I "nail" it to the board as I throw knives over her head. She bends down to her hands and knees at, which point I take her

22

hand, pull her forward and she stands up leaving the skirt behind. And there she stood, on stage at Monday Night Magic in a wonderful, sexy leotard. The crowd roared. And then when Astrid was standing behind a six foot by four foot piece of paper through which I was about to throw six axes along the sides of her body I called out,

"Astrid, are you there?" All I know is she yelled back something from the other side of the paper veil that made those in the audience that understood German laugh quite loud. To this day I'm not sure what it was but I've been led to believe it was suitable for an adult audience only! (She only admitted to calling me silly but I think it went further than that.) Then, to her surprise, as she dropped the paper and stepped forward it to reveal she was safe and unscathed,

I was standing there with a bouquet of roses in my hand. The look on her face was priceless. It's the thing that great stage moments are made of.

The audience let out with such a resounding applause all we could do was smile from ear to ear. And then there's the producer of Monday Night Magic's response when he saw me spinning The Wheel prior to throwing. You could hear him on the audio tract of our video. It went something like this, "Oh my God. Did we get a copy of his liability insurance?" Yes, I did give it to him before the show. At that moment he forgot everything and was probably trying to remember if he brought extra underwear.

The theatre was filled to the maximum. A funny point worth mentioning was that my sister-in-law, Mary Beth (aka JAFFN), was there on a first date with her boy friend Steve. She pulled the scam off so well by suggesting they go to a magic show for their first date. Little did he know The Great Throwdini was her brother-in-law. She revealed the truth to him during intermission when I walked over to her and said hello. The look on his face was priceless. They're still together. I guess I didn't scare him off. He's a wonderful guy and always brags to his friends about my exploits.

Our performance was over. We relished in the moment of our standing "O" and we ran off stage back to the dressing room. WE DID IT and we were unscathed.

Following our act was the headliner for the evening, Simon Lovell. Simon is highly recognized internationally as one of the best sleight of hand magicians with a deck of cards, as a comedic magician and a stand-up comedian.

(As fate would have it, Simon actually stood in for one of my assistants when I headlined for Monday Night Magic at Tannen's Magic Camp. I was called to fill in for someone and I couldn't get an assistant in time. Simon agreed to stand in and was so graciously named "Simone" for the evening. It had to be one of my funniest shows ever. I was doing my thing and Simone was doing his with impromptu comedy. It literally brought the house down and to this day I have magicians who saw the show come up to me to tell me

they were in the audience). Astrid and I snuck through the alleyway of the theatre for seats in the last row. I clearly remember Simon's first few words, "Now THAT'S a REALLY hard act to follow." Astrid and I smiled from ear to ear. We smiled, smiled and continued to smile as we envisioned ourselves on stage. Perhaps it's best to say we glowed. What a difference it makes from the other side of the lights! From on stage you barely see people in the front two rows as bright spotlights literally blind you as you look toward the audience. You know they're there but you can't see them. Then you look from the audience side and the performers are so beautifully lit up. It's cool; they see us, we don't see them. Anyway, as we watched Simon's performance he got to the point where he brings up someone from the audience to tie him up in a straight jacket. Of all the people in the audience he picks Astrid's boyfriend, Joachim. To this day I'd swear that Joachim thinks Astrid and I set him up. We had nothing to do with it, honestly. The banter between the two of them was marvelous. Astrid and I enjoyed the moment immensely.

After the audience left we had to dismantle everything. That meant disassembling the board and The Wheel plus repacking boxes of knives and our costumes. It's a big job and certainly not appreciated by anyone that's never done it. Joachim, Harry and Joe all helped. Boards, hardware, knives, clothes, etc. etc. etc. were all carried out to my Hummer and packed in tightly. The six of us, (my wife Barbara and I, Joachim, Astrid, Harry, and his wife Joan), all went back to the hotel in downtown Manhattan, just blocks from the former site of the World Trade Center. We all shared the same room and as you might expect, knocked off a reasonable amount of adult beverages!

The next day we got up as early as our hung-over heads would allow. We had a pretty nice breakfast and headed off for an entire day of walking around downtown Manhattan. We went to the World Trade Center site, Chinatown, City Hall, the Village, and up to Hogs and Heiffers, a famous biker bar in the meat district. The one thing that stands out was a man talking on a banana phone. That's right; he was holding a real banana to the side of his head and was talking into it as if it were a phone. It was sad. He was as he was holding an imaginary conversation with himself.

That about does it as my memory is fading fast. That fateful Monday, however, shall remain in my mind forever. Thank you for reliving it with me. I'm sorry you missed the show.

27

A Day On Broadway – The Art of being a knife thrower's assistant from Lady Astrid's point of view

Germany

How everything started

"The knife thrower from America is coming to Germany and he's going to do some shows over here! Can you imagine working with him on stage?" This was the first I heard of this from my boyfriend Joachim. I had no idea what he was planning and for how long. At that time, Joachim and I were about to finish our exams at the university for a Master's of Arts degree in philosophy. It was my primary focus in life. Little did I know about his "friend" from America; the knife thrower.

I knew that Joachim was interested in throwing knives. In retrospect, I guess, I wasn't totally surprised at the visit of an American knife thrower. But believing I would have the courage to work as his target, standing at a knife thrower's board – that was something new! Sure, doing unusual things has always been a part of my personality. OK, why not seriously think about it?

As a young girl, I was always fascinated by sideshows and circus people. In fact, for two years I lived in an old circus wagon, not far away from an isolated farm. Later on, when my two children grew up, I went back into civilisation and joined a colony of artists, where everyone lived side by side. From time to time, they put on theatre and circus shows for the children. Authenticity at that time was "doing it, being a part of it." So I practiced juggling, and I also had fun doing archery. But soon most of those ambitions were lost in the passing of time. With the forthcoming visit of the knife thrower these old fantasies turned up again, with the real prospect of carrying them out. But having ideas and a vivid imagination are one thing. Reality is another.

Anyway, I was able to give a serious reply to Joachim's question. I was at least able to imagine, at that moment, being part of the show. How would things really turn out? Would I be able to do it? I wasn't sure at all. But it certainly raised my curiosity. How would I know how it felt to have my head framed by 14" throwing knives? Thank God, I didn't know yet about those tomahawks and machetes. Little did I know they were about to come flying towards me soon enough...

Soon enough, David Adamovich, alias The Great Throwdini, his assistant and his box of knives arrived at Frankfurt Airport. Actually I'm not in the habit of being shy, but as my spoken English wasn't very good I was rather quiet that day. Later on I learned that David misunderstood my behaviour and thought that I was afraid of him. I wasn't afraid at all!

As Joachim had to go to the university in the afternoon again it was my part to be the hostess. I spend the rest of the day with David and became quite friendly with him very quickly. Right at the beginning I got to know him as a careful man and appreciated his friendly personality.

Well, David wouldn't have been the Great Throwdini I was soon to know if he hadn't set about rehearsing right away. Coming home from work the very next day, I found myself in the middle of the "warming-up" of two knife throwers; he and Joachim. I wasn't sure if I was at least allowed to take off my jacket, but it was clear that the two gentlemen were eager to learn how I would do my job on the knifeboard as a target-girl. Anyway, they gave me the time to put down the jacket, because the knives had to be thrown close to my body. I was about to have a "crash course" on being the knife thrower's assistant. Rule one: The target-girl is the star of the show and she has to be aware that the stunts depend on her. She is the one that is standing in the middle of the limelight. All eyes are focused on her. Rule two: You must not move!

Theory and practice are two entirely different things, however. Now I went right into practising.

I was positioned at the board and a video camera was started as an objective pair of eyes. The first knife was thrown followed by the questioning look of David. As I showed composure he went on throwing. "If you look at the knives, you'll move! Don't look at the knives coming! Look into my eyes!" David said. One knife after the other was drilling into the board until my body was framed by two straight vertical lines of knives. The stunt was repeated a few times. We critically watched the video. It was kind of strange to see myself in such an unusual role! Anyway, I learned that my eyes had been blinking as the knives were thrown, in particular as they made a loud thud when hitting the board. We went back rehearsing and I started to control my expression. After a while I was even able to smile while being surrounded by knives. As I showed no fear David started to throw the knives close to my body. My blinking didn't stop entirely at that time, but at least one problem was solved. Even if I wanted to move I couldn't as I was perfectly framed to the board with knives just inches on each side of me. We had a break and it seemed that the throwing was over. That disappointed me as

I wanted to go on. Neither David nor Joachim could imagine that I was eager to go on rehearsing. But I was! From this moment a great team was born.

The next day I had my last verbal exam at the university. David and Joachim were to pick me up afterwards. We developed several ideas for our show at the university. Our guest, Professor Dr. David Adamovich from America, would present himself at our graduation celebration as a knife thrower. But the fact that he would invite me to stand at the board as his assistant was an idea which fulfilled us with joy.

Now a costume had to be found for me. David loved my brown-black high cut leotard from the first moment, Joachim selected the boots, and I added the tied blouse. Because I had to look elegant at the party at first, I hid the leotard under a white skirt with blue pattern. David noticed that the printed marks on the skirt were the Chinese symbols for marriage. A witty coincidence if one knows that David is a minister and marries couples in America.

The day of our performance was at hand. A lot of preparations had to be made and the guests were to arrive soon. I still had to put on make-up and my blouse was crumpled. David astonished me by taking the blouse out of my hands saying he would iron it. That is one of the nice memories I have and I learned that David can use a piece of steel even if it's hot.

The stage name

Of course we wanted to show David some of the sites here in Germany. Mainz lies on the river Rhine, but the time was too short for taking a boat and going down the river. So we took Joachim's old Mercedes and went along the roads near the river. Every few kilometres you can see castles and ruins beside the river. In the

Astrid

Middle Ages Germany was divided into several small Marks, small Earldoms and Principalities, all with their own currency, weights, measures, and armies. And each of the sovereigns had to profit from boats passing along the Rhine. Thus the river was closed on every border and duty was raised, even if by force. David found this fascinating and inquired about the castles he's heard about in German tourist books.

Our next stop, therefore, was to visit the castles. The monuments were built not in the valley, but at the summits of the rocks on each side of the Rhine. Much to my surprise Joachim and David wanted to conquer and explore the castles — even if it meant climbing the rocks and many levels of the castle. During these strenuous climbs within the castles David and Joachim conjured up many stories to amuse each other. Obviously their imagination was terrifically inspired by the surroundings. While we scaled the narrow natural stone stairs, which rewarded us at the top with breathtaking views across the Rhine valley, Joachim and David made up dark stories about "Warlords" and wild battles. Sometimes while coming down through dark cold passages leading into a musty unknown, the stories were lightened with some romance.

What were all the struggle and battles for, if not for the beloved or adored woman? The noble lady of the castle must be rescued from captivity and torture in those dark castle dungeons of her enemies.

In that way originated my stage name: Lady Astrid. Not satisfied with that, Joachim and David subsequently embellished it even more by adding "The Lovely and Daring" as a prefix.

The first performance

Our show had the desired affect as the audience was held on the edge of their seats during the entire performance. The distance as

35

usually found in a circus had disappeared completely. Those attending were taken by surprise to find a knife throwing performance with me being the guest target girl standing at the board. The knives being thrown were absolutely real and were even examined while on display before the show began.

On the one hand, I lacked the experience from such a short preparation time. On the other hand, I was very excited of course. It was my task to respectively hand my "master" his knives as his assistant prior to my stunt. In addition it was necessary to collect the knives that were thrown from the board. After the second or third stunt one of the knives was stuck in the board very deeply. I incorrectly pulled out that knife by using my index finger as a fulcrum and cut my finger open right down to the bone. The blood was instant and a lot. I didn't feel the pain at all because one thought David told me somersaulted in my head, "The target girl makes the thrower look good." I had the sinking feeling that my failure would spoil his show and his reputation. I quickly squeezed the wound together with the thumb of the same hand trying to suppress the bleeding. I didn't succeed completely due to the running blood, though. Throwdini noticed the blood and by the look on his face it appeared that HE THOUGHT that he might have injured me. However, I didn't want our performance to be interrupted and I whispered to him: "The show must go on." It didn't work, however. A thick terry towel and a decent pressure bandage were applied to save the day. We quickly continued with the next stunt.

Despite the mishap the show was successful. My self-esteem had got a deep psychological scratch, though. But both the scratch and the cut healed quickly within the next days. We repeatedly laughed about the situation very much afterward and about my two wonderful men, Joachim and David, who both felt my behaviour rather courageous and highly professional. David has said many times that the success of the show was due in part to my bravery in this awkward situation.

Public reactions

David and Joachim reviewed the video recordings of the show on the same night. I did justice to my tiredness and rapidly fell off to sleep despite the ruckus the two of them were stirring up. Of course the next morning was filled with so many stories about what everybody had experienced. In that way the events of the day before took on a new life. The reactions to it came almost immediately — a high tide of enthusiasm and joy I found rather amusing. The time of reflection had none-the-less hit me for the first time. At first this name, The Lovely and Daring "Lady" Astrid. I am from a long-established craftsman family. My father had done genealogy and found out that our ancestors had owned a castle in Switzerland. But this was a rural fortress in the country and only a part of the descendants turned to the skilled crafts before spreading themselves throughout the world, including the village in which I grew up. We only recently learned that the brother of one of our direct ancestors had immigrated to the state of Pennsylvania in the United States. I have never considered myself a "Lady." I paint pictures, plant carrots and cabbage in my home garden, brought up two children at the same time and earned a living by cleaning and teaching in night schools. When David visited I was just completing my graduate studies in philosophy at the university. But I don't feel born into the aristocracy.

A "Lady", this is a quite special title and reserved for a woman with high status and fine manners who is protected and provided for.

I have, however, worked with people who were addicted to drugs;

chased rats out of old houses, renovated the walls in a farmhouse, cut wood so as not to freeze to death in winter. It was strange living up to the title, despite it being a stage name.

A fan club had arisen around this "Lady" in a very short time. In many conversations I have tried to understand what fascinates these fans so much about this personality. For me it must have been an element only men can share with each other. I would come to understand it only much later, and then to be revealed by another woman.

It was time for David to depart. But we knew there was more to come. He asked me if I would be his assistant for his first appearance at Monday Night Magic in NYC in only a few months. I had no reason not to believe him. I wondered, however, why he wanted me to assist him in such a professional show after performing together just once before in Germany.

Ceasefire

My telephone bills went sky high and for the first time I learned to appreciate the Internet. The distances are hard to bridge from continent to continent. I had also to improve my linguistic proficiency. David explained he had no talent what so ever for a foreign language and said he would never get beyond hello and good bye in German.

David was "obsessed" with two things: 1) his first appearance on a well known cabaret stage in the Off-Broadway performance of Monday Night Magic, and 2) "Das Rad." One of the few things he learned really well in German was "Das Rad." In English, "The Wheel of Death." Throwdini had given us videos with different showmen who performed The Wheel. He was so intent on performing it at Monday Night Magic that he would literally dream about it day and night. Obviously he had already planned to use me as his Target girl for Monday Night Magic. I could only laugh about what seemed such an absurd idea.

At this time David and I were almost daily in contact via e-mail. You might wonder if it was love. I can tell you from the bottom of my heart that it wasn't the kind of love you might have in mind. At that time I had already been with the man of my life, Joachim, and had no further ambitions. But never-the-less there was a strong emotion I felt while working with David. I can only speak for myself that as a Target Girl there is a kind of love-relationship between the thrower and his assistant — that special bond that develops between two people performing a high-risk act. This relationship starts with the contact of the eyes after the thrower positions me at the board and lies far beyond a kind of superficial eroticism. It is a relationship of deep trust and understanding. It is a relation which presupposes the deepest mutual confidence.

One fine day about a month after his departure David e-mailed, "Set out and get yourself some plane tickets. We're on." It was such a shock that this idea was now becoming a reality. I have taken on different temporary jobs because my further professional career still wasn't clear at the time. We say in German, "So the Lady wasn't hung with gold at that time." Two plane tickets to America weren't at all in the budget of two starving wretches like Joachim and I. We were, at that time, two graduate students who just finished our studies.

I was still in close contact to our philosophy professor. There is an essay by a relatively unknown German philosopher with the title "Entangled in Stories." A result of his scientific examinations states that, "You are your own history." Is there a better story one can tell to their children and grandchildren as this one — that their mother or grandmother has appeared as a knife thrower's assistant on Broadway? What was I thinking? What would they think? Would they ever believe me? Would they think it was just a wild story in the imagination of an old lady recollecting the past? How could I possibly say no to this opportunity? It was, more than anything else in my life, destiny.

The decision was made. There also was the consideration that Joachim and I had slaved like dogs to get our studies done. The right time for a vacation was now! We were in the travel agency and had paid for our tickets. There was no turning back, despite the most unusual feeling in the pit of my stomach.

Now Joachim and I were facing the reality of the of the 7 hour flight across the Atlantic ocean to NY. Anyway, Joachim and I got there safe despite a rather restless flight; even though we had been crushed between an ancient Asian woman who could neither hear nor understand me and a permanently sleeping man I wouldn't want to disturb, we had to endure getting kicked in our backs by kids who were brought up without any parental authority.

America

The first contact

To really care for someone means, for me, to go on exactly from the point were you have stopped when seeing that person for the last time. No problem with David!

Now this was the Promised Land! David had picked us up from the Airport in his Hummer. The first thing I noticed was how familiar this foreign land seemed to be. Sure, the highway signposts were green, not blue as they are on the German Autobahn, the white frame houses had much free area around all sides being fundamentally different from the German style. The way people were standing in public places talking to each other made me feel like home. Another thing I remember were the many pennants in the American national colours of red, white and blue. I found them everywhere and soon

Astrid and Throwdini
Rehearsing in Freeport/New York

came to realize it was a strong American pride following 9/11.

"Unfortunately the bottles of water have got very hot in the car! Simply imagine it as very thin tea," said David. I smiled. He wouldn't have got a good laugh in England with that one I thought. But the heat accompanied us for all the days of our stay, interrupted by a quite peculiar coolness caused by the air conditioners in the houses. I don't recall much about this first day any more except the bright atmosphere in David and Barbara's home. They live along a canal and there home has many large windows, generally open all the time. There was a lot of light and always a pleasant breeze — despite the heat. But wait! Of course! The refrigerator really caught my attention. My son had an unusual wardrobe in his first room in a student apartment-sharing community. It was a pink-coloured

American refrigerator from around 1950. I have always admired this one because of its enormous size. But this cooling and freezing combination in David's refrigerator really astonished me. I would value the comfort of having ice cubes in all thinkable sizes within the next days. All I had to do was push a button and there they were.

I am not sure any more, whether it was the strain by the hard work of rehearsing with Throwdini or the fear relying on cup after cup of coffee to keep on working. My cigarettes would suffice at home but David was always making comments to me about this. This crazy American really cared about my health, right from the day I arrived. He made comments about my cigarette consumption in Germany but now he was relentless. I think he said smoking was dangerous to my health. Here I was, practicing with him as he threw hundreds of knives just inches from my body and all he would do is comment on how unhealthy my cigarettes were. Hello in there…those are REAL knives. I always appreciated his confidence and I trust in his skill. He told me over and over that the most important thing to him was his assistant's safety, and he really meant that.

Then work started.

Becoming a knife thrower's assistant

The spacious patio in the Adamovich's back yard led directly to a jet-ski ramp, immediately catching my attention. During the day big tourist ships come into the canal and dock just across from were we rehearsed on his deck. The first step, however, in becoming a professional target girl was my walk to the wooden boards standing upright, turning round to face the thrower.

Throwdini's knife board was considerably smaller than the one which we had built for him in Germany. The difference in size was a little unnerving at first as I had imagined that the knives would be thrown closer to my body. Sure, they had been thrown close before, but now they had to be even closer since there was less room.

We started with the stunts I already did in Germany: holding a paper plate in which five knives were thrown, standing straight up while the knives are thrown in two vertical lines to both sides of my

Astrid and Throwdini

body and up to my head, standing sideways while three knives are thrown behind my back and bending backwards over the three knives to give way for the rest of the knives to outline the front of my body as I bent backward, exposing my throat. I always had to count the throws not to leave the board early and into the flying knives. After each stunt I made a step forward and took a triumphant bow with Throwdini.

The knives thudding into the board, the counting of the thrown knives began to set its rhythm within me. And after a while I really started to dance in my high-heeled boots in response to that rhythm.

I was dancing and we started to adapt ourselves to each other. But my dancer was leading me from a several meters of distance. Even though I was only wearing my high cut leotard the heat and strain made me sweat.

We took a break and David and Joachim went on building "The Wheel" to accommodate my size. As I was soon to find out, The Wheel had to be modified for me. After a glass of water with crushed ice the training went on. Two little ancient wooden tables are part of Throwdini's stage equipment; a candlestick is on it and various materials which we needed during the show lies in the little drawer. His knife suitcase filled with the different throwing tools sat on yet another table. During one of the opening stunts I had to throw a burning knife to Throwdini. He caught this one and threw it in the middle of knives thrown before. It exploded with a loud bang. This was not as easy as I had imagined. First it's gasoline soaked handle had to be lit and then I was to toss it in a way for him to catch and immediately throw. I was so afraid I'd misthrow it and cause him to catch the burning end. This would be the first stunt in which I was involved on stage. To make a mistake at the beginning of the show wasn't a good idea.

Apart from the different positions to be taken at the board there were also other things to rehearse: the appearance on the stage, the suitcase, lightening the candles, opening the box and getting knives, axes and machetes and uncovering the knifeboard were just the beginning. I had to learn the entire act in a just a few days. "Move your hips. Dance. Take a shorter way to the board. And always

Astrid and Throwdini
Ducking down for the last three knives

smile." I had two strict instructors with both Joachim and Throwdini watching every move I made. It was an unbelievable wealth of details which I had to keep and to take into account within the short time to rehearse. Then after hearing everything else over and over I'd hear, "Don't stand with your back to the audience!"

Our performance got into shape. "Can you do a headstand?" Throwdini asked me. Sure I could. But doing a headstand in the privacy of your living room and doing it in front of a knife thrower who is about to throw knives between your legs are two entirely different things. The stunt with the headstand had to be perfect. The

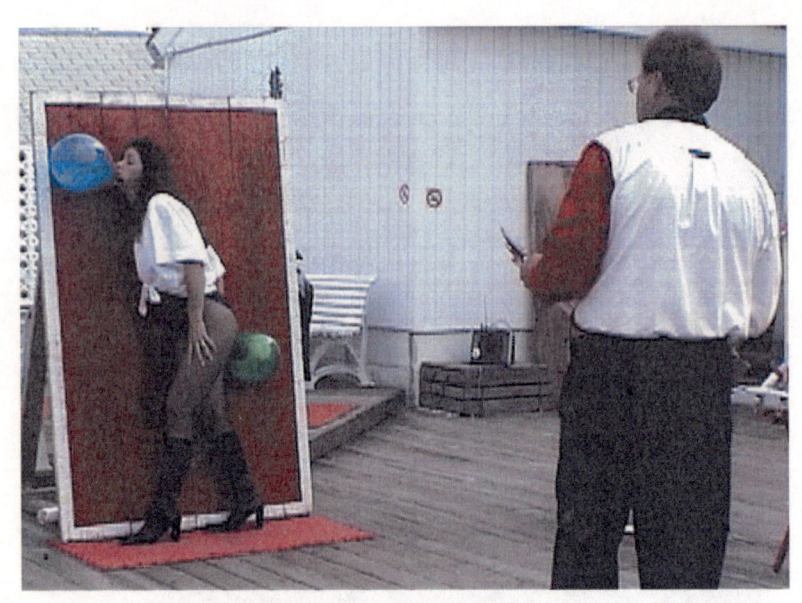

Astrid and Throwdini
Rehearsing the "balloon stunt"

boots were not to make a loud noise if they hit the board. Throwdini corrected the attitude of my elbows. He needed sufficient room to put the knives next to my head. The risk of an injury was always there but Throwdini kept it as little as possible. Finally the headstand stunt turned out well. The knives were thrown from the bottom, where my head was, up to my legs. When the knives reached the highest point I had to open my legs in straight V shape to the outside, fitted in into the rhythm of the hitting knives. The last knife lands in the upper third of the board between my legs. And then after all that I'd hear, "Get down without stumbling or twisting, stand, take a bow to the audience – smile!"

Unexpected applause

There were several stunts in our performance that we did with

Astrid and Throwdini
Axe in flight

balloons. One of these tricks Throwdini particularly liked. I was standing sideward in front of the board holding a puffed-up balloon

47

in my mouth and another behind my back at the same time. However, he didn't hit the balloon behind my back as I anticipated; he intentionally missed it. In my first surprise I took the balloon out of my mouth and yelled at him "Du Tollpatsch!" which more or less means "You clumsy creature!" Throwdini and Joachim were laughing hard and I knew he had done that on purpose. Right at this moment we knew how that stunt had to be done on stage. (I remember the audience at Monday Night Magic laughing almost as hard as the two **men** did during rehearsal.)

Anyway, I took the balloon between my teeth again, straightened up waiting for the knife to break it. The rubber shreds popped and whipped into my face as in the case of a chewing gum bubble. Grinning and rolling my eyes I spat out the remains. In the next stunt three balloons again served – beside me – as targets once again. One was jammed between my legs, the other two I was holding in my hands with my arms crossed in front of my chest in a way that the balloons came to lay on the wood just a tiny space away from my shoulders. Three knives were thrown and finally the last balloon between my legs was hit. I held my arms high in the air and, like going for applause, I called out: "Throwdini!" And indeed applause came from a distance. The people on the big tourist ship had watched our rehearsal. First I felt embarrassed but a few moments later it made me feel good.

Much to Throwdini's chagrin a cigarette break and more ice water were in order. He and Joachim fiddled with the ball bearing construction of the wheel as I had my cigarette. "We must put you on the device now." Maybe it would have been better to take a whisky with ice. This was the moment of my first spin on the wheel. Throwdini took my hand like a real gentleman and helped me to step on the narrow foot pedestal on the wheel. My boots were strapped across the toes with leather loops. Joachim observed with a critical eye. With a pushing movement I pressed my shoulders under the irons that would hold my shoulders in place. Snapped closed the restraining belt around my stomach. "Now I'll turn you once slowly and carefully," said David. He touched the iron over my left shoulder and set the wheel in motion. My long dark hair fell in my face, the iron harness press very hard into my shoulders and

Astrid and Throwdini
Double handed knife throwing

little clouds in the sky passed over and over. Throwdini asked, "Does it feel alright?" Yes sure, apart from the fact that the flesh of my shoulder was getting cut by the harness, everything else was just fine. The harness had to be wrapped in additional padding and tape before our next spin. There was still no whisky. We went for a second

Astrid and Throwdini
Bending backwards while beeing outlined

attempt. The upholstery had helped a little bit. Now the speed of the rotation was increased significantly. My long hair whipped above the external edge of the wheel; the spinning pressed me against the iron fixtures. On the right and on the left beside my pelvic bones were another two long handles for me to hold. I needed to counteract my whole strength around the pressure outwardly. Sure, I wouldn't have fallen off the wheel, but the pain in the shoulders was quite violent. After several spins, David stopped the Wheel in the upright position. The straps were opened. Everything was turning in my head. The world was still rotating. Without Throwdini holding me I would have fallen right on my face to the floor that appeared to still

Astrid and Throwdini
Getting Astrid from the board

be moving BUT it wasn't, it was only my head that didn't know the difference. Now I needed no more water, but a scotch would have been just fine.

Other issues with The Wheel arose at this point. It seems that my centre of gravity and the centre of The Wheel needed to coincide. Without correction The Wheel would spin faster downward and slower upward. Joachim and David immediately set out to correct the problem. They devised a plan to attach weight plates behind The Wheel at the level of my lower legs to solve the problem. It did. We were soon back to spinning and throwing. My head and stomach were not happy.

Here we go again.

The next day David took us to a store where he was to buy some equipment we would need for our show. After a short journey over dusty streets he parked his Hummer in front of the store and ran right into business. The asphalt was glowing hot and exuded the typical smell of heated up tar. David was well-known here and introduced Joachim and I as his friends from Germany not forgetting to mention that the dark haired German beauty would be his new assistant. I would have killed him for that, but the dealer provided such a wide range of weapons and ammunition that I couldn't decide which one to take. Anyway, I experienced what happened again and again in different situations later on: we were greeted with a warm welcome and in a most friendly way. After talking to the dealer about all kinds of things and about his plans for the future David picked up the ordered goods and, among other things, a set of throwing knives for Joachim.

Back again we took some time out and everybody took care of their own business. Barbara was still at work in the clinic and would be back in the afternoon; David was working in the kitchen while constantly answering phone calls and e-mails at the same time, Joachim was working out in David's gym constantly telling me that the weights weren't sufficient. I went on working on my costume.

David wanted some red coloured additions to my costume, so that our appearance looked more uniform. He himself wore long black tails, a white shirt with red bow tie and a red cummerbund. Due to his red accessories my long black satin skirt still needed some red trim. He also wanted me to wear a red satin ribbon around my neck and my skirt had to be modified to fall off easily. As if it would be the easiest thing on earth we became a part of the family. David's mother helped me to modify the costume and brought out her sewing kit and red ribbons. She and I talked about her vacation to Germany years ago. So much has changed.

After the worst midday heat had faded we went on with the rehearsal. We repeated the stunts we had done the day before critically checking our progress. Now the throwing became faster and in addition we practiced a new stunt with the machetes. I had no problems with the knives flying towards me or even the axes. Sure, I had to get used to the axes. The made a different sound when hitting the board and they seemed to penetrate the wood deeper, but nevertheless in a softer way than the knives. However, I would never get used to those machetes! They are very long monsters; the blade is more pliable than those of the stiff accurate throwing knives. In conjunction with the heat and the wind on the wooden planks they raised some very different feelings. For me they have something snakelike and generate a bright tone while striking on the wood. They are springy after the hit and I do not know why, but they have reminded me of big handsaws. The hardness and clearness of the knives inspired some confidence for me. The knives stick or they don't, there is nothing in between.

In retrospect, the effect on the audience when we did the stunt with the machetes was terrific. But we had to stop practising with the machetes because it was getting windy and their big surface was extreme sensitive, so the precision of the throw would be affected.

Astrid and Throwdini
Outlining the Lady with two lines of knives

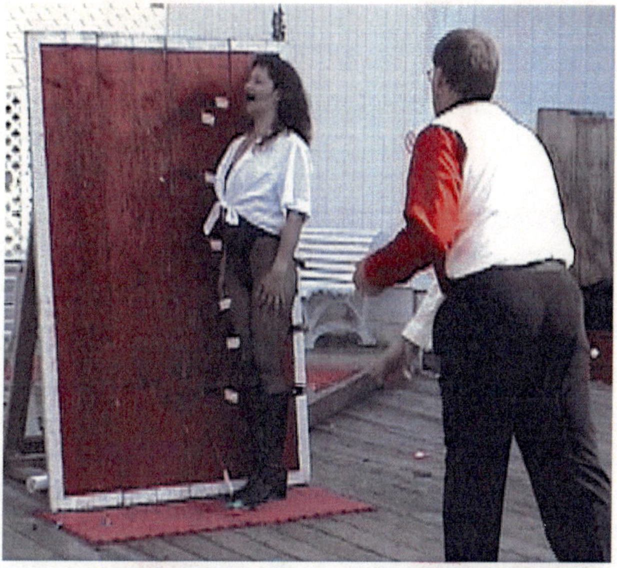

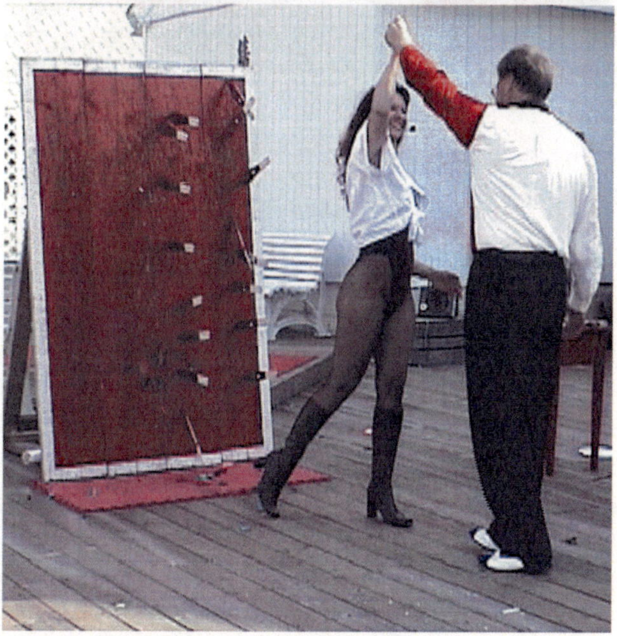

Ok, let's rather face the "Wheel of Death" again!

Meanwhile David and Joachim had fixed the irons of The Wheel fitting my size. I climbed up, was strapped in and turned for some revolutions. The centre bearing was all right and ready now, my stomach wasn't. Now was the time for the first attempt with the knives. The wheel rotated with high speed this time. The fact that knives were thrown around my body was of minor importance at that moment. "Are you all right?" Finally the straps were opened and I reached out for something or someone to hold on to not to loose consciousness.

The whole stunt was on video. When checking it we arrived at the conclusion that the throw rhythm of the knives and the speed of the wheel required modification. In addition, one could see that my head was acting in an unnatural way; it appeared to push to one side. My aversion and my nausea had reached a high point. The time to the show was closing in on us and I knew the need to do more work was necessary. "Ok, let's do it again" I said. "Try to smile" Joachim said. "Try what?" I yelled at him. It was the first time ever I saw this muscle packed guy backing up in fear off me. I smiled, at least as long until the wheel started revolving again. My day was done. My body was exhausted and I had to find my composure again. David and Joachim were in a good mood and went on throwing knives together in the backyard. I went for a cigarette in private.

The Wheel of death became a part of our rehearsals now and the routine was almost complete. Now we could start to work on other show elements. I improved my dancing style and I started flirting with my thrower again. The flirting started while I was brought to the knifeboard and with a smile and short nodding I signalled my thrower that I was ready to get outlined by his knives. At the end of each stunt David took me away from the board turned and twisted me around leading me to take a bow in front of the audience.

It was always of the greatest importance to David, that our routine didn't turn out to be a kind of submissive act like the grim torturer and his helpless victim. As a matter of fact I didn't play any role but being myself. It was a kind of love story, maybe a strange kind of love story, but nevertheless a story about the relationship of two people that care for each other and have a deep trust in each other despite the danger we would present to the audience for a few minutes. Maybe Jamy Ian Swiss, one of the producers of Monday Night Magic, has found a very true description for our show when he said "It's a snapshot of America, it's sex, and crime and rock'n roll." It was sexy, it was dangerous and it sure was shaking to the bones, but it never was degrading, neither for me, nor for David, nor for anyone who watched the show. David and I were performing as equals on stage. That's why David insisted that I introduce the "Impalement Arts" portion of the show. He carefully scripted a few short sentences in which I would tell everyone that his job was to miss me although I was his "target." And, believe me, the audience was eager to find out if all that what I was telling them would really now happen before their own eyes!

Despite David's focus on The Wheel of Death, there were other stunts of significance. A stunt I considered difficult is the "Double Blind" stunt in which David throws, both masked and hooded, to sounds I make by tapping a knife on the board. My responsibility in the success of this stunt was substantially greater than with the other stunts. After I had put the mask and hood on David I had to give him signs where the knives should hit by knocking on the board. For me finding the right throwing distance to the board seems to be the real art beside the throwing technique. I handed the knives over to him and he could indicate his readiness only with gestures. The visual contact was lost and had to be substituted by the knocking on the board. I caught myself nodding at him when I was standing at the board in the right position. This was senseless of course because he could not see me. However, it showed me that I had started to internalize my role as his assistant and partner. I had to find my correct position on the board without the possibility of any correction from him. The stunt ran in such a way that I had to stand precisely in the middle of the board with a knife in my hand which pointed upright with the point to my chin. Using the knife I had to randomly knock on the right or left side of the board only inches away from my body. Throwdini threw his knives directly at this perception of the sound, three knives on both sides of me. The last knife had to be placed in the middle of the two knife rows about at the height of my chest. That is, I had to knock the signal for the seventh knife directly where I was standing as I jumped out of the way. Bang, went the flaming and firing knife he threw! (The handle was soaked with camping gasoline and the knife was fitted with a blank 32 calibre bullet). Throwdiniiiii!! We did it!

The individual stunts came together to become a routine. Now and then we had to do some corrections but in general it was all right. I was even able to smile as the wheel slowed down giving Joachim a big grin when David offered me his hand to step down. I was always grateful for the fact that The Wheel came as a climax of the routine as it made me feel giddy. If that weren't enough, David announced that we would add a final stunt to follow The Wheel. My smile faded faster than the sickness. Stepping down from the wheel, doing some steps and taking a bow to the audience was now at the border of possible. One more stunt? Impossible! "Michael Chaut, a producer of Monday Night Magic, wants me to do some magic on stage," said David. There was to be a card trick that David introduced with someone from the audience picking a card early on in the routine. Now this card would appear again at the end of the performance in connection with another stunt. I was hidden behind a paper curtain which I had to unroll to completely cover my body. David would throw six axes through the paper screen into the board behind it, hopefully missing me. To make it clear for the audience that I was really still standing behind the paper screen he wanted me to say a few words in German. "I haven't the faintest idea what she

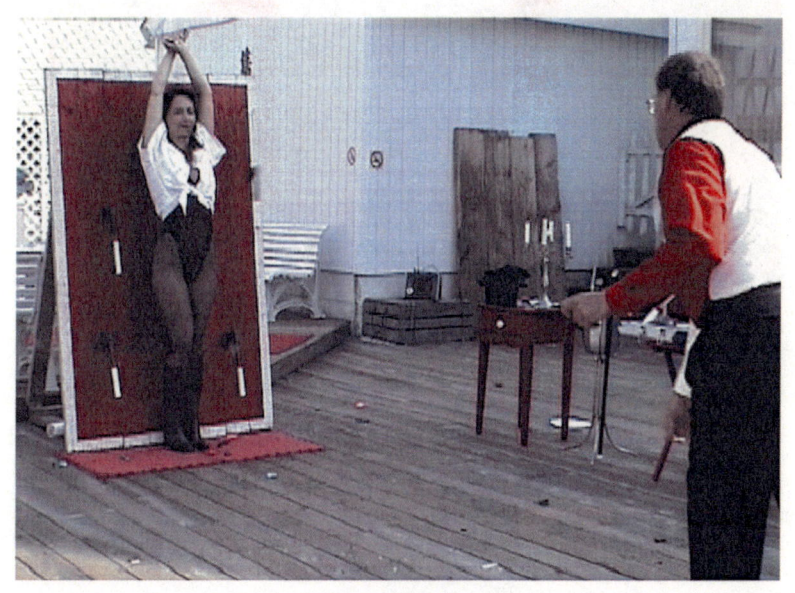

Astrid and Throwdini
Axe throwing

is talking about but I know she's there and she'd better be in the middle," he said, getting a good laugh from the audience. Well, he still hasn't the faintest idea what I said, but I also haven't any idea how this playing card the spectator had drawn appeared between my lips as the paper screen was torn off revealing me surrounded by axes.

Astrid and Throwdini
The headstand

There is a life before the show

I was stiff in the back and my limbs hurt from all the strenuous work. It was time for a little holiday! I would never have expected how wonderful Barbara arranged our stay in Freeport! With a sure feeling for what might be of interest for us Barbara and David made us acquainted with the everyday life of America and came up with some great events. We also went fishing by the sea. Long fishing rods were put into the sand and we would just sit there telling stories to each other. After a while I just wanted to watch the sea, feel the wind and taste the salt that was within in the air. The sun on my naked skin felt so good and made me forget about my sore muscles. I didn't feel any impulse at all to change this pleasant eased condition. Just lying there being stroked by the warmth below coming from the hot sand was all I wanted to do. Feeling very high-spirited this morning David and Joachim didn't give up until they'd lured me into the water. Anyway, it was all right. We went out for a swim, laughed and created all kinds of nonsense. For the first time I had the feeling of being on a vacation.

Astrid and Throwdini

David doesn't just throw knives around women, he also works. So it matches his romantic soul that he marries couples. Therefore, we could even watch some real American wedding ceremonies. There were many utensils in white, a lot of pink flowers and a little gazebo for the ceremony by the waterfront on the deck behind David's house. It seemed strange to a German girl and I wondered how the working place of a knife thrower could become a sacred place within just a few minutes. Well, it happened. But enough of romance and leisure time, we had to get back to work.

Dress rehearsal

We had our last rehearsals and were going through the whole routine again in our minds. Had we thought of everything? Will we stick to the order of the stunts? Did my dancing match the music? Was everything considered very thoroughly? DID WE MISS ANYTHING?

The dress rehearsal would be in the late afternoon. David had invited some relatives to watch our routine. His wife Barbara would see the whole of the routine for the first time. Barbara is the woman behind the scenes. She patiently listened when David came up with new ideas and plans in his own impatient way, and always cooled him down by giving some good advice. She was the observer in the distance and always kept the overview. She also knew all the girls David had worked with and was aware, like no one else, of how important this show was for David. Her judgement was most important to me.

The dress rehearsal started. The several pieces of music were the measurement for the duration of each stunt. Movements and music had to fit together perfectly. Everything worked just fine and to my surprise it was no problem for me to move and dance and even smile in front of a live audience. The spectators were watching the act with tense concentration. They knew that their judgement would soon be needed. Just the music and the vague sound of the hitting

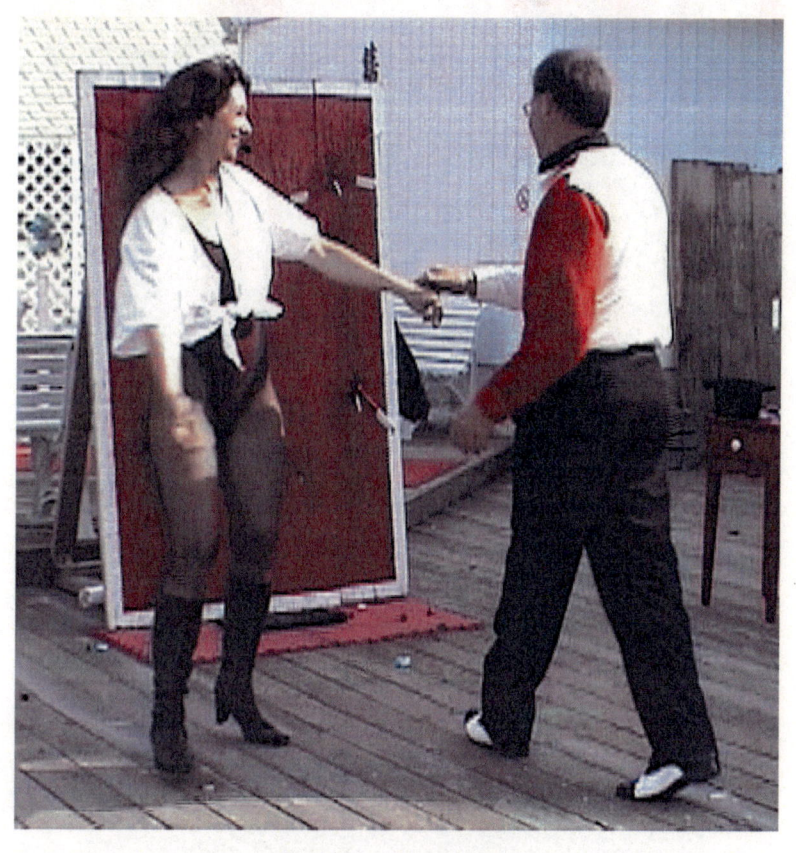

Astrid and Throwdini
Going for more MAXIMIUM RISK

knives were to be heard. David introduced the target throwing stunts and then it was my turn to introduce the audience to the "Impalement

Astrid and Throwdini
Rehearsing The Wheel of Death

65

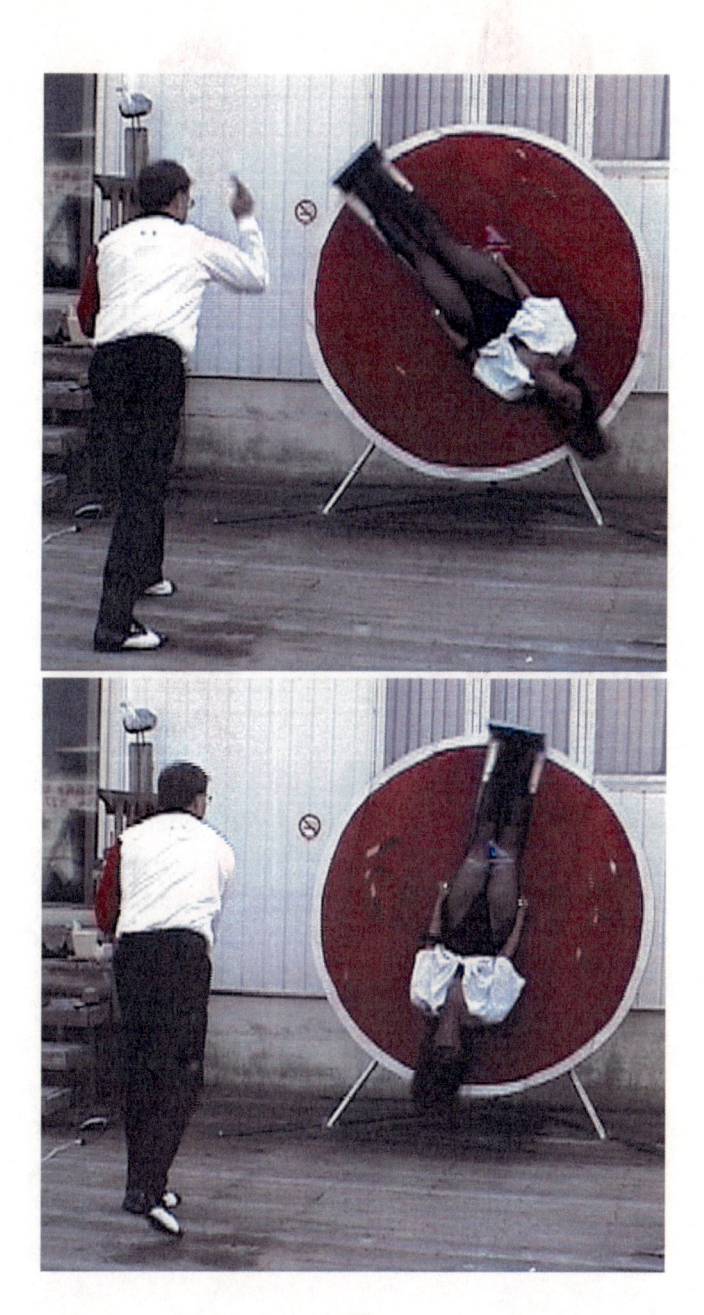

Arts." The audience listened intently to my explanation, eager to see the action that followed. Finally, The Wheel! I didn't know this stunt was first introduced to the American stage by a German couple. It gave our appearance a special significance for me. All the knives had been thrown perfectly as I whirled strapped to the revolving disk. I climbed down with a smile as my nausea had almost disappeared. We finally did the last stunt and the spectators were having fun watching us making our little jokes to each other. When the paper screen was torn off I stumbled as I stepped out. I knew that was something to be avoided on the big night to come. David picked me up and we did our last bow in front of the audience who gave us a big round of applause. I looked at Barbara and saw her standing there clapping her hands full of joy and enthusiasm. Ok, that was all I wanted to see! Broadway, here we come!

The Big Day

Preparations

So many things had to be taken care of. The stage properties had to be collected, I packed my leotard, the red ribbon I would wear around the neck, my high heeled boots, my make-up and finally the hair dryer. Most important was the hair lacquer because my hairstyle would have a lot to go through. I had polished and painted my fingernails in a deep red the evening before surprised that none had broken within the last days. But the fishnet stockings were still missing! As a matter of fact I preferred the black nylons with the sexy seam in the middle but during the rehearsals they had dissolved into a series of runs. David wanted me to wear fishnet instead, because they probably wouldn't tear during the show. I guess that wasn't the only reason why he insisted on me wearing them. But anyway, his wish was my command and we went shopping at last minute. Did

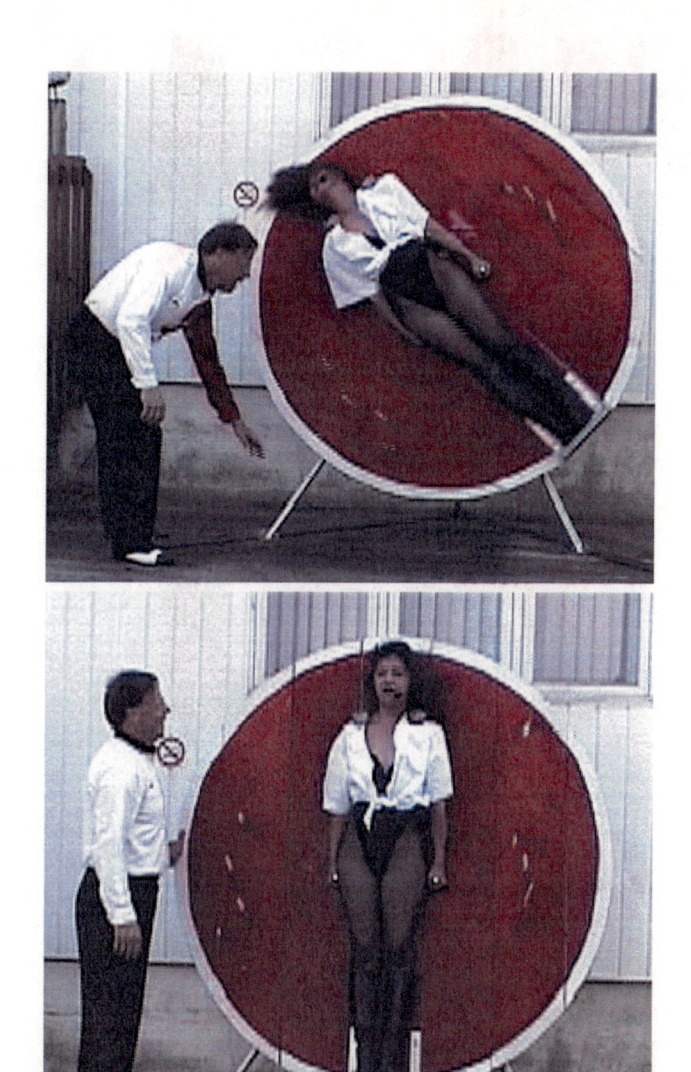

"Are you ok?"

we have the lighter for the candles? David looked for it. It wouldn't be the last time it was missing. David and Joachim were finally taking apart the board and the wheel and loading them into the Hummer. I began to feel the first signs of a migraine. I feared it would only get worse.

Astrid and Throwdini
Throwdini presenting the Lady unharmed

    Everybody was still busy doing or getting something and then almost in response to a secret signal we were all sitting together in the Hummer and the journey had started. Luckily I was sitting in the back of the car and didn't have to talk a lot. So many things were going on in my head. Despite the heat I felt cold. The migraine was getting fiercer and I was wondering what might have caused it to appear just at this moment. Attacks often begin with tension in the back. There would have been enough reasons for that within the last couple of days. But why right now? I treated, as unobtrusively as possible, the nape of my neck with an ointment. David started joking and sometimes turned back and smiled. I felt no desire to

Astrid and Throwdini
"Are you ready for the next stunt?"

joke about anyone or anything and gave rather brief answers. The ointment had been of no use. So I had to take a painkiller to block the rush in the early stages. At home this might have helped, but here and now? My left hand started to get numb and felt like it was going dead. Slowly panic rose in me. I know only too well how these attacks develop, but I hadn't experienced them in such an acute state for many years. Outside the car the landscape was passing by. I don't remember one single detail. Hoping that nobody would notice my misery I tried again to go through my notes which described the stunts of the show. Little flashes of light made it impossible for me to read. I knew that I wouldn't be able to speak anymore within the next few moments. The annoying thing was that I knew how the attack would develop but could not predict how long it would take. I was waiting for the headache to come. I knew it would be hell, but I would at least know how to handle it. The worst case would be that I would faint on the stage! Well, great! In that case I would have lived up to my stage name. Isn't that the way one fancies a real lady, fainting in the face of danger? This was another fine mess I'd gotten myself into!

New York City

At the hotel

At one point in the journey, David, full of enthusiasm, turned to me telling me that we were just passing Broadway. Meanwhile my headache had started. I was pale and felt like I couldn't either move or speak. This was the first time that I felt like running away, but even thinking about that seemed impossible because of the pain I was going through. The hotel had excellent air-conditioning. I felt freezing cold, wrapped myself in a thick blanket and snuggled into a little ball on the sofa. My stomach started churning and there wasn't even the slightest chance that I would be able to eat. I hated the situation and I also started to hate myself for such silly behaviour. But it wasn't silly at all. I was experiencing a very bad migraine. Sure David and Joachim noticed that I didn't seem to be all right. But I told them that I was just tired. There was no time to argue about it because they had to go to the theatre to load-in all the equipment. I could only hope that the time left would be sufficient to get myself through the worst part of the migraine. Then Harry and Joan arrived at the hotel.

Astrid and Throwdini
The Lady behind the paper screen

Harry is a really nice guy; maybe the kind of guy you would imagine to be a real quiet country farmer. His little belly showed me that he had tasted the sweeter side of life. Harry went off with Joachim and

David to move the heavy board and the wheel and to build them on stage before the show began. Joan, being the opposite of her husband, started to bring the house down. Getting over my initial surprise, I got to know her better. She stands for Harry as a Target Girl and also her son started knife throwing when he was a little child. Joan showed a sympathetic understanding for me and the situation I was going through at this moment. She explained to me that she also had stage fright before a show and that this simply would be part of the situation. Stage fright? I know what stage fright is! I didn't have any stage fright. I was just freezing to death and suffering a terrible headache! "Come with me little beauty! I know what's good for you now" she said. Joan went to the bedroom with me and massaged my back. Wow! That really helped! And after a hot shower I started to feel better. Could it really be stage fright? No, never! No way!

Monday Night Magic

I was so grateful to have Barbara and Joan on my side. They managed everything for me and kept telling me not to worry. We all took a yellow cab to the theatre and got there about one hour before the show was scheduled to begin. The straight board and The Wheel were already on stage. David and I didn't have a chance to rehearse in the theatre as the brief time we had would be spent dressing and applying make-up. I walked across the stage for the first time and somebody led me through mysterious secret passages behind stage to the dressing rooms. The walk way was dark and cluttered with all kinds of strange props and theatre lights. In some places the stage lights were shining through the walls and scenery from the show that played in the theatre during the week. (As I found out, Monday Night Magic rented the theatre on the "dark" night of the theatre). Behind a door small stairs were leading up to the dressing rooms. It was eerie to move from the dark passages to the well-lit dressing rooms. On one side there was a counter crowded with used cups and cold drinks for the performers. On the wall hung an

Astrid and Throwdini
She's like an angel!

old automatic coffee machine to brew tea or instant coffee. On the opposite from the table was an upholstered armchair of indefinable color. On in sat an elderly magician repeatedly shuffling a deck of cards. We greeted each other with a tip of the head without talking. I later realized his reserved look was because it was rare for a female to enter this inner sanctum of Monday Night Magic performers. Almost all the acts were males who performed by themselves without assistants.

A lanky young man entered the room, stopped in the door frame, leaned against it and said, "Are you OK?" Much later I found out that he was also one of the artistes of Monday Night Magic. After our appearance I would see him live on the stage. He was Simon Lovell, the headliner of the evening. We pursued a little small talk. Then, finally, I saw a known face. David appeared. "Could you help me with my bow tie?" he asked already dressed up in his tails. I found it so amusing that with all his talent and skill he couldn't figure out how to tie his own bow tie. I also noticed his hidden strain. "Well, you must change quickly," he added, "We're on in less than half an hour." Now I noticed a little door beside the armchair. Two ramshackle steps went up to the dressing rooms with rows of make-up mirrors. It was my turn to do make-up and change. I pushed David and everyone else over to one side. I enjoyed the dressing room and the make-up mirrors as though I were there alone, despite having to share the room.

There was not much time left to get dressed, or may I say undressed. I put on my fishnet stockings, leotard and boots. My unusual way of getting dressed did not seem to bother the two men. Oh well, not completely. David couldn't hold back a mischievous grin. Everything went smoothly now. My hands didn't even tremble while I was putting on my make-up. David's appreciative look let me know the results were good. I wouldn't see Joachim before our appearance on stage. He was already sitting in the audience. David accompanied me down, directly behind the scenery. A young sound engineer was busy whispering into a small wireless microphone that sent cues to the control room at the back of the theatre. Our music cues were briefly clarified from the instructions David made in advance. The final instructions were given. No turning back now. We listened to Jamy Ian Swiss' introduction, waited for the music to begin and David said, "That's it. We're on. Let's go."

Astrid and Throwdini
"Is that your card Sir?"

In the limelight

Stepping out of the twilight behind the scenery the floodlights on stage blinded me. I wasn't able to see the audience but nevertheless I had the intense feeling of being watched by many eyes. "Move your hips!" "Dance!" Start lighting the candles!" The commands appeared in my head. I had had two good teachers. The little flame jumped out of the lighter, but the candles were new and did not burn immediately because the fine wax layer had to melt first at the wick. The music was running ahead. I opened the case with the knives, took them out, turned around and showed the large throwing knives and machetes to the audience. While Throwdini went on stage I uncovered the knifeboard by pulling down the cloth that was hiding the red wood. Throwdini's appearance provoked a loud applause. We did the first stunts, the so called "Target Throwing". Throwdini threw perfect "Bulls eyes" in the middle of the paper plate I was holding. I assisted collecting the thrown knives and passed of the objects he needed. I didn't throw the flaming knife perfectly but Throwdini caught it fine and threw it flawlessly. During the first stunts my skirt was nailed to the board, stepping forward I stood in front of the audience now just wearing my boots and the high cut leotard with the little blouse. I heard a loud whispering coming from the audience, some were even cheering. It was somehow clear to me that most of the spectators seemed to like my Target-Girl outfit. Now it was my turn to introduce the next part of our show. I moved closer to the edge of the stage in front of the audience: "Ladies and Gentleman! The next part of MAXIMUM RISK will be the Impalement Arts! The master's job is to miss his target! The target …. is me!" After having said that a real firework of throwing knives started in front of the audience. I was moving free, dancing to the rhythm, flirting with Throwdini and the audience while his knives outlined my body. He now threw the knives real close. One throwing knife even touched the bow of my blouse just inches away from my chest. The audience went crazy. The machetes and axes were flying around me. The headstand, the Blind stunt, everything went fine. And now: The Wheel. David, leading into the stunt, told the audience about the history of the Wheel of Death. It was perfectly quiet in the

Astrid and Throwdini
"Why, yes of course!"

theatre as Throwdini took my hand leading me to the Wheel. I stepped up and was strapped to it. There was still no sound to be heard. Throwdini started to turn around the wheel until I was rotating with high speed. Later, watching the video of the show, I could hear someone shouting "Oh, my God!" Eight knives were thrown to the revolving disk I was on. Throwdini stopped the wheel from turning. There was no headache anymore, no strange feeling in my stomach. We did The Wheel! I was still on the little platform of the wheel with the straps around my boots as just cheered with my right arm in the air: "Throwdini!" If the audience was crazy before they now went nuts. The relief of seeing the Lady surrounded by knives but save and sound went into a big applause. Is it possible to do another stunt after that? Yes! The stunt with me as the target behind the paper screen! The audience was laughing at the little jokes we did. Even though the stunt was also dangerous we all, the audience, David and me enjoyed the last stunt which was now the perfect encore. I stepped out of the paper screen, where the axes where thrown in, holding a playing card in my mouth. "Is that your card, sir?" David asked the man who was involved in the little magic trick. The man nodded and said something I couldn't understand because the applause was going up leading into a standing ovation. There the Lady stood, holding a big bunch of roses in my left hand and David on the other taking a deep bow in front of the still cheering audience. Our show was over, but the applause went on as we left the stage. I remember Jamy Ian Swiss saying before introducing the next act: "I have seen a lot of knife throwing acts, but this was by far the best I have ever seen!" What more can I say? Well, maybe just one thing. OK, Joan, you were right. It was stage fright!

Back in Germany

Our little adventure would probably have soon fallen into oblivion if Throwdini had not put a video with clips of the show on his website. I received e-mails from fans from all over the world for weeks, even still months, after our appearance. Of course I was surprised, but also proud to hear that many wanted to see me in the limelight again.

"Weren't you afraid while being the target of a knife thrower?" was probably one of the most frequent questions I received. If I had been afraid, I would not have done it! Of course the skill of Throwdini was a basic condition for the fact that I appeared as his assistant. A friend from America wrote: "For me your real courage lies within your openness for the other person and your ability of complete devotion". This ability to be able to dedicate oneself confidently to the other person is probably a part of the fascination of a knife throwing act. If this ability is shown by a strong woman, the fascination is probably even bigger for the spectator. A woman who wrote to me noted that I reminded her of Emma Peel, alias Diana Rigg, from the TV series The Avengers: A nice intelligent woman who nevertheless, however warlike, remains female and elegant. I particularly love this comparison, especially because Emma Peel has already been a big role model to me from childhood onwards.

During the next year there wasn't a lot of spare time. Joachim and I published scientific books and he wrote his thesis in philosophy. One day Joachim started to throw knives again. The board used for the first show in Germany still existed. He practiced and became really good. One day he asked me: "Can you think about standing at the board?" This question came quite unexpectedly for me. The show with Throwdini had almost become history, but the old memories still came up again. So, knowing that Joachim was able to do it, I positioned myself at the board. The knives were smaller than those which Throwdini had used. They came thrown in with such a force that it almost took my breath away. My eyes blinked, and I wobbled about, just as though it was the first time I had ever stood at a board for a knife thrower. On the other hand, I felt how confident Joachim had become. Nevertheless I was still used to the way of throwing a knife, that I had experienced with David. It is remarkable how much the throwing expresses the character of the thrower. David and Joachim are two totally different persons. David is the gentle one, the providing person, the doctor of the medicine and the adviser, the man in tails with the black-and-white patent leather shoes. Joachim is the fighter with iron discipline, however, with extreme sensitivity and care. Anyway, we had taken the first step, and now and again we spend an evening with knife throwing, practising the Impalement Arts. The whole thing was rather amusing as we didn't take it too seriously. We came up with a few ideas and gags; elements from which a little show could be built.

The relation between my thrower and me as the Target Girl is also different with Joachim than it was with David. David has been the professional and the teacher. I could co-operate with him because I completely trusted him and generally didn't have any trouble following his advice. He was never haughty, but always gave me the feeling of being important and special. With Joachim it works on another basis. We go with each other. The partnership in which live now has an added sphere of activity. Nobody is ahead of the other. Each brings their own specific abilities and we share our common experiences.

Events forced us to take a break from working out the preparations for our little show. My father died, my mother had to undergo an operation and I also had some minor surgery.

Time passed and I started to throw knives myself, and developing a little skill, I enjoyed it for a while. But again I couldn't go on because other things became more important. Joachim went on throwing and tried to get some bigger throwing knives over here in Germany. This had failed. So he ordered the knives made by Harry Munroe. Joachim found enough time to go on throwing and get used to the new professional knives. Bit by bit everything had returned to normal. Our little performance is still developing, even though it is still hard to find the time to do it. When, some days ago the knives no longer made that hard dry sound when sticking in the board but rather softy and vaguely sank into the wood, the message was clear: We need a new board. We are not taking risks with a little show that doesn't sound good.

Do two persons really have to throw knives at each other to express their relationship?

Certainly not! But Art renews itself again and again and is successful when it reflects the reality of life. Truth is real in those big subjects that engage people: love, eroticism, perfection, fertility and death. Life is extremely dangerous. Within ourselves, over and over again, we need to conquer our fears creatively.

At the end I would like to insert a quote from Stanley Brion who wrote to me some time ago: "What you want is to create an illusion, a mystical interaction, which expresses the essence of human life. You are holding in your hands and in your minds, the power and the discipline to control the action."

A Short Philosophical Essay on the Art of Knife Throwing
by Joachim Heil, Ph.D.

"Good stories make you feel you've been through a satisfying, complete experience. You've cried or laughed or both. You finish the story feeling you've learned something about life or about yourself. Perhaps you've picked up a new awareness, a new character or attitude to model your life on."
(Christopher Vogler, THE WRITERS JOURNEY)

When I met Dr. David Adamovich for the first time in Germany, I was strenghtened in my opinion of him which I had gained through previous letters and talks with him: In his art of knife throwing, he aspires more than just the presentation of sheer ability on the stage. As his performing in tails already suggests, he wants to set himself apart from the image of the cowboy or the western hero. He has kept pointing to the fact that for him, thrower and assistant are equals, that together they constitute a unity for the audience. What David wants and aspires is to present knife throwing as a form of theater and as a form of art.

David and I have had long talks about what thrill a knife throwing show could hold for an audience. However, we have not reached any definite conclusion. For sure, part of the pleasure the audience gains derives from the knife thrower's dangerous play with the life of his beautiful assistant. Yet what remains still unexplained is the meaning that this fascination holds for the one who watches. If this fascination had its origin simply in the face of pure danger, and if what was at stake was simply the kick, then the bungee jumper or the mountain climber would experience the danger of death much more authentically than the audience of a knife throwing performance

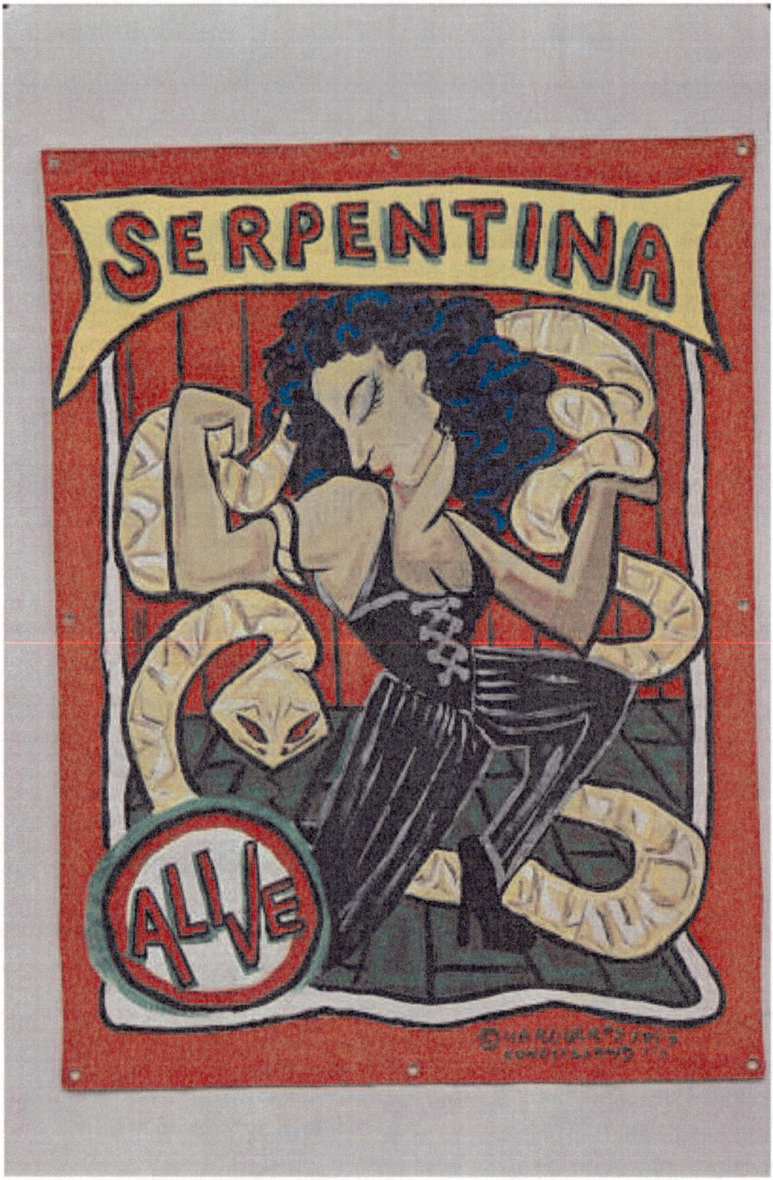
SERPENTINA
ALIVE

ever could. The figure of the knife thrower is older than the adrenaline junkie in the fun society. If it was only a matter of sexual appeal, of seeing a beautiful girl in the hands of her tormentor, then this fascination would be trite, and other media would provide greater satisfaction. What is it anyway that intrigues us about this danger which a knife throwing show presents to us on the stage? How must this danger be communicated in order to be intriguing to us? Is it actually possible to elevate knife throwing to a form of art? Isn't it exaggerating to speak about art in this context? These are some of the questions I want to deal with in this essay. I do not pretend to give final answers here. Rather, I want to try to give some hints about what a philosophy of knife throwing, or more accurately, a philosophy of the circus, might be.

There is no such thing as a philosophy of the circus. One might refer to the philosophy of one or another specific circus performance, just as one speaks of the philosophy of an enterprise. But this is not what I mean here. It is one thing to put down arguments on a flipchart and to discuss whether or not to call a brand of toilet paper "Happy End" to increase its sale. But it is another thing to seriously consider the things we are doing and why we are doing them in an existential way. Philosophy deals with the big, eternal questions of mankind beyond all empirical possibilities of answering them: Is the soul of man mortal or immortal? Is human will free? Does God exist? Philosophy does not necessarily want to find an answer to these questions, but it wants those questions to be posed in the first place. For philosophy, those questions define the essence of what it means to be human. Philosophy traces those big questions in the particular and also on a small scale, in ordinary everyday life. It traces them in art, in mythology and in the stories we tell. Thus, if we want to outline a philosophy of the circus in its essential features, we have to borrow from the philosophy of art and the philosophy of the myth. This way, we can get an idea of what a philosophy of the circus might reveal.

Therefore, in the following, my explorations will be divided into three parts. First of all, it is necessary to examine and to define the figure of the knife thrower. Where do we find the origin of this character? However, I do not want to investigate his origin historically, but rather derive it philosophically in free association from the figure's meaning.

Subsequently, I will ask about the meaning of art from a philosophical perspective. What meaning and what sense does it have for us to be watching a tragedy, a drama, a show in the theater? This leads to the third part of the investigation, that is, to the philosophy of the myth. What meaning do the myth and its heroic stories hold? In the last part, I want to link my results with each other. Here, I will answer the question, at least in a rudimentary, tentative way, of the essential and philosophical meaning of a knife throwing performance which is staged in an artistic and dramatic way. Let's turn to the figure of the knife thrower himself.

Broadly speaking, the knife thrower is a persona, a mask (compare lat.: *persona* – mask), who has at his disposal various abilities to master an object or a tool – a knife, in this case. He is the initiate who has perfected his abilities in years of training, in order to now present them in playful lightness. However, he is not a skilful artisan who employs his abilities for a rational end, like to sustain or increase life. What he presents is the complete opposite of what we would normally expect of a rationally acting person. The knife thrower employs his abilities in order to present the senseless and the absurd. He does not use his abilities to protect or to secure life, but to endanger it and to confront it with death. He plays with the life of another human being and evokes shiver and fear in the audience, with the audience at the same time also feeling a certain kind of pleasure.

At this point already, an element of great importance for philosophy emerges: the element of purification, or rather, catharsis.

Aristotle remarks in reference to the tragedy in his POETICS:

> "Tragedy, then, is an imitation of an action that is serious, complete, and of a certain magnitude; in language embellished with each kind of artistic ornament, the several kinds being found in separate parts of the play; in the form of action, not of narrative; through pity and fear effecting the proper purgation of these emotions." (Aristotle, POETICS)

What Aristotle talks about here is the element of purification from frightening states of excitement by living through these states of excitement from a distance. At this point, it is crucial to note that what the knife thrower is doing no longer seems to be senseless when it is seen under the aspect of theater and tragedy. Rather, it's about a certain purifying experience which is to be evoked in the audience. I will elaborate on this in a moment.

The character and the action of the knife thrower seen from a rational point of view, however, are absurd to the extreme, even senseless. The figure of the knife thrower unifies rationality and absurdity.

I am now claiming that this element of unification of rationality and absurdity applies to all figures of the circus. The lion tamer, the snake charmer, the tightrope walker, the sword-swallower, even the magician – all of them, they possess highly distinguished rational abilities to direct nature (their own and/or a foreign nature) or certain objects. Yet their actions from a rational point of view are absurd

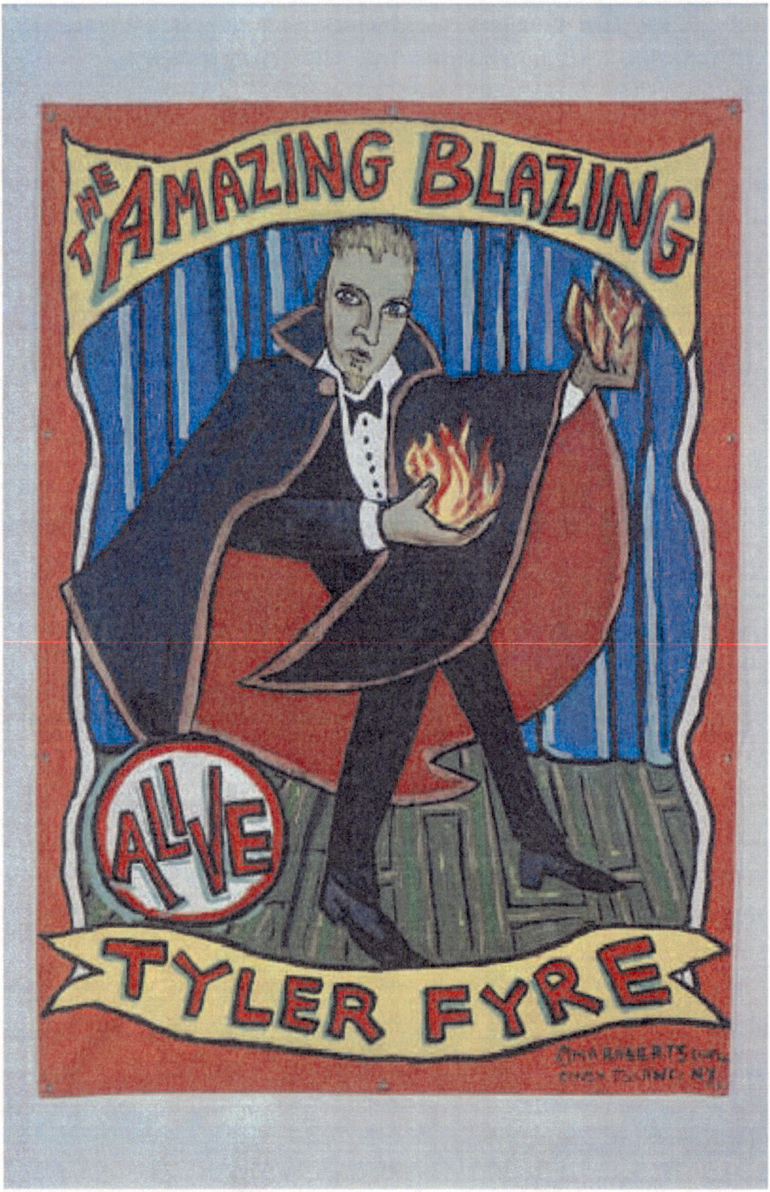
THE AMAZING BLAZING
ALIVE
TYLER FYRE

and even senseless. Senselessness seems to be the sense of their action. Crucially, death always plays a certain role in all this. It may be more obvious in the case of the knife thrower who plays with the life of his assistant or the magician who seemingly saws up his partner's body than in the case of the juggler, who in the worst case lets his balls drop to the floor. Yet in the figurative sense, the balls falling on the floor also announce the death of the juggler and his act. Even if the juggler may not injure himself when his act fails, he dies an inner death, which the audience experiences and suffers as well.

The meaning of death for the circus act leads to the probably mightiest figure of the circus: the clown. All figures of the circus are masks of the clown. The clown is the mask behind the mask. He is the prince of death. Why is this so?

The clown in the figure of the White-faced Clown is the authoritative, serious and intelligent leader of a collective of clowns, and he has never existed as a solo artist. The White-faced Clown wears an expensive, elegant and glittering costume made of velvet and silk, knicker-bockers to his knees, white silk stockings and elegant shoes. On his head he wears a simple cone-shaped cap. His face and neck are painted in white, mouth and ears in red in contrast. Usually one of the eyebrows is emphasized, being painted in black.

I cannot elaborate on the individual attributes of the clown in this context. However, the mask of the clown reminds us of nothing other than a ridiculed death mask. The clown appears as the dead who ridicules the living and presents their true face to them. The clown appears in the mask of an exaggeratedly painted and decorated dead person.

The White-faced Clown has his origin in the *mīmus albus* of the antique comedies and ultimately in the harlequin.

Originally, the harlequin was no joker, no buffoon as we know him from the *Comedia dell'arte*, but the prince of death, the *hariloking*, "king of armed forces," the king of the dead and of the empire of death, who with his "wild army", the *familia Herlechini* or *maisnie Hellequin*, traveled the world at the well defined and always limited time of the festivals of transition. He was a mythical figure who led a band of demons across the sky on ghostly horses, terrifying peasants with their attacks in the dead of night. The absurdity of his action may explain how the buffoon could evolve in time from the figure of the harlequin as the king of the dead. The harlequin appears, as do the dead on Halloween, at certain sacred times, not only to scare, but also to admonish atonement and to bless. A figure that terrifies and blesses at the same time seems absurd. And this absurdity even increases. In his book Die Masken des Dionysos, Stephan Grätzel emphasizes the close connection between harlequin and Dionysus (see Grätzel 2005, p. 158ff.). Dionysus as the god of antique cult festivals was one of the chained gods. Dionysus, or rather the statue of Dionysus, was chained in order to show that his power was limited to certain sacred times. For Stephan Grätzel, the harlequin's captivity is repeated in his squared pattern. This absurdity, not only in his behavior, but also in the representation of a mighty god, was interpreted as silliness during Christianization, the original meaning being lost and the harlequin transformed into the buffoon. The cult of the chained gods as well as the festivals of masks and visits are all about a temporary unification with the realm of death and the underworld. This feared time is the origin of all richness and renewal of life. The harlequin displaces the existing order, admonishes the remembrance of the dead and blesses where the unification of the dead and the living, the integration of death into life, succeeds. The harlequin represents the reconciliation of life and death and the vision of life in its wholeness. He transfers life to a higher order, one which can appear as absurd only from a rational perspective. This is the original meaning of the clown and his actions. His act has a cultic, theatrical and dramatic character. We will see later on, that one can also find this very aspect in the knife throwing act. In an even more pronounced way than in the modern clown's act, the knife thrower's act exemplifies the cultic aspect of initiation. Like the White-faced Clown, the knife thrower appears with his entourage. He carries out the cultic act of initiation on his assistant. Again, this is about the reconciliation of life with death, the apparent death of the one who is to be initiated and her rebirth on a higher level. It is of no importance whether or not the assistant is fearful or whether she dies. To the contrary, this aspect would be harmful to the whole enterprise. Decisively it is the way in which the audience experiences the show. We will also see that the purifying effect of the performance can only be achieved for the audience if there is no real confrontation with the assistant's terror of death and her actual death. Only a good knife thrower is also a good dramatist, and only a good assistant is a good initiate; or, to put it differently: only a good knife thrower and a good assistant are good clowns.

Let's move to our second set of questions. What is the meaning of art for philosophy? Why can one speak of the circus act, or knife throwing act respectively, as a form of art? Why does the knife thrower depend on a dramatic performance? Why isn't it enough for him to prove his abilities without endangering the life of his assistant?

Let's recall that the knife thrower and his assistant, like all other circus artistes, display something which makes no sense from a rational point of view. There really is no specific interest which drives us to watch their performance. We might justify our interest by referring to our pleasure or entertainment, but this interest does not aim at a specific rational end. It is really an interest without interest, or rather, a pleasure without interest. This is exactly what Kant claims concerning the aesthetic and concerning art:

> "Taste is the faculty of estimating an object or a mode of representation by means of a delight or aversion apart from any interest. The object of such a delight is called beautiful." (Kant, THE CRITIQUE OF JUDGEMENT)

What does that mean? What does Kant mean when he speaks of a delight apart from any interest? He wants to suggest that we experience a certain freedom when we're looking at a piece of art, that is, a freedom from the rational coercions of being. This is the core of Immanuel Kant's aesthetic theory.

However, Kant does not develop a theory of art, of the theater or the drama in the narrow sense, but uses the concept of beauty or art in the context of cognition. Cognition, or the possibility to make judgments, means first of all an activity of reason. Here, certain concepts are brought to a synthesis, like in the judgment which Kant uses as an example, "The rose is red." Here, reason itself determines that this object, or this rose, contains the predicate, the color red. This judgment may be reconstructed and checked, and in this sense, it may claim an inter-subjective, or objective, validity.

According to Kant, however, we do not only make such determining judgments in which an object is attributed with certain clearly defined properties, but we also make judgments where this is not the case, so-called reflective judgments, like "The rose is beautiful." There is no unambiguous definition of beauty and yet, Kant says, we make this judgment with the demand that others share this judgment; they may not consent unconditionally, yet they can consent in principle. If we are aware of the fact that we cannot expect a general consent concerning the judgment of the beautiful rose, yet make this

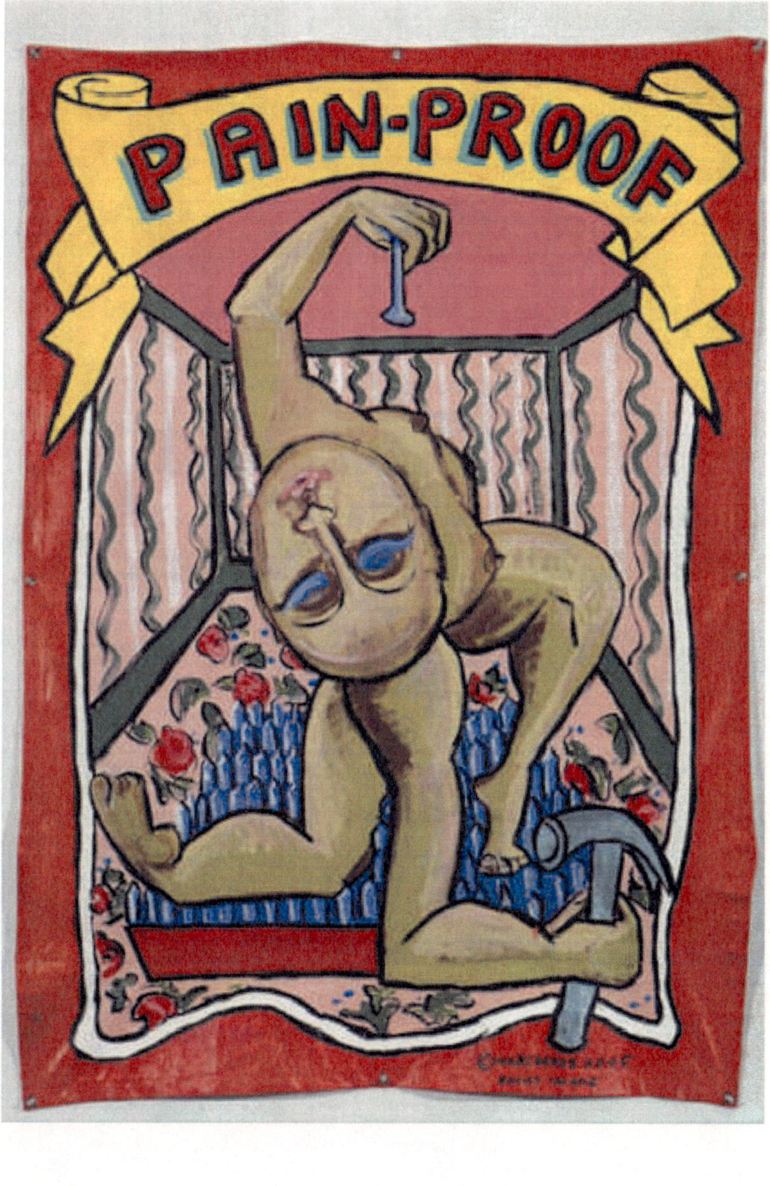
PAIN-PROOF

94

judgment with a certain claim to universal validity, then the question arises what it really is that we want to communicate to others.

Kant expresses this in the following way:

> "If, then, the determining ground of the judgement as to this universal communicability of the representation is to be merely subjective, that is to say, to be conceived independently of any concept of the object, it can be nothing else than the mental state that presents itself in the mutual relation of the powers of representation so far as they refer a given representation to cognition in general. (Kant, THE CRITIQUE OF JUDGEMENT)

Thus, if we make a judgment of taste, we do not make it, according to Kant, in order to transmit the object itself, or our opinion concerning this object. Rather, this judgment is about our mental state.

This is so, Kant goes on, because

> "…the cognitive powers brought into play by this representation are here engaged in a free play, since no definite concept restricts them to a particular rule of cognition. Hence the mental state in this representation must be one of a feeling of the free play of the powers of representation in a given representation for a cognition in general. (Kant, The Critique Of Judgement)

Thus, what is communicated is not the object, but the subjective state of free play of our cognitive powers, which give pleasure; they are free, as they are not limited by the rules of reason. Though the object of judgment, in this case the rose, cannot simply be omitted, it is rather the medium of communication for this freedom; yet we do not communicate the rose or its apparent beauty, but our cognitive powers' state of free play. This state not only claims subjective, but also inter-subjective validity and in a way insists on expression. In the aesthetic judgment, or the free play of cognitive powers, human freedom shows itself and freedom insists on expression.

What does all this have to do with the circus or the knife throwing act? Nothing really at first sight, were it not for the German writer and philosopher Friedrich Schiller.

Schiller takes up the thought uttered by Kant in The Critique of Judgement. Here, the idea reveals itself that man's humanity does not only show itself in the cases in which he calculates and combines in a more or less simple way, but that he becomes truly human in those instances when man is able to transgress the boundaries of reason and to fill the pre-existing form with life. In the approach of Kantian aesthetics Schiller recognizes an educational task which has to be executed further.

Communication, not experience of beauty, is crucial for Schiller as well, but apart from that, it is important for him to recognize that the lightness of play is not simply an addition to the seriousness of life, but rather, that this is what makes life possible in the first place.

Thus, Schiller writes in his 26th LETTER ON THE AESTHETIC EDUCATION OF MAN:

> "Extreme stupidity and extreme intelligence have a certain affinity in only seeking the real and being completely insensible to mere appearance. The former is only drawn forth by the immediate presence of an object in the senses, and the second is reduced to a quiescent state only by referring conceptions to the facts of experience." (Schiller, LETTERS ON THE AESTHETIC EDUCATION OF MAN)

The highest stupidity and the highest intelligence coincide for Schiller in the way that they dissolve in the factual, in the real, without transgressing it, even though they may look at this factual from different, possibly also learned, perspectives.

Stupidity and intelligence reveal reality for us in the way that we are bound in it by our concern for survival and our fear about finitude and mortality and in that we are therefore unable to develop a sense for merely beautiful appearance. Stupidity and intelligence leave us to become, in the original sense of the word, creatures unable to dissociate ourselves.

It is only play, the beautiful appearance, the drama, which enables us to gain the kind of distance we need in order to develop a sense of reality, a sense for that which reality means to us.

Beautiful appearance is the way in which we learn to understand the things, reality and ourselves in ways that transgress stupidity and mere reason. Therein lays the task of aesthetic education.

> "In short, stupidity cannot rise above reality, nor the intelligence descend below truth. Thus, in as far as the want of reality and attachment to the real are only the consequence of a want and a defect, indifference to the real and an interest taken in appearances are a real enlargement of humanity and a decisive step towards culture." (Schiller, LETTERS ON THE AESTHETIC EDUCATION OF MAN)

Thus, stupidity and intelligence are for Schiller the results of a lack of understanding of beautiful appearance. Being bonded to reality, we are worrying, fearful creatures, yet we have to learn to regard reality in such a way that we can become aware of what we really are and what this reality means to us in its totality.

> "That which first connects man with the surrounding universe is the power of reflective contemplation. Whereas desire seizes at once its object, reflection removes it to a distance and renders it inalienably her own by saving it from the greed of passion." (Schiller, LETTERS ON THE AESTHETIC EDUCATION OF MAN)

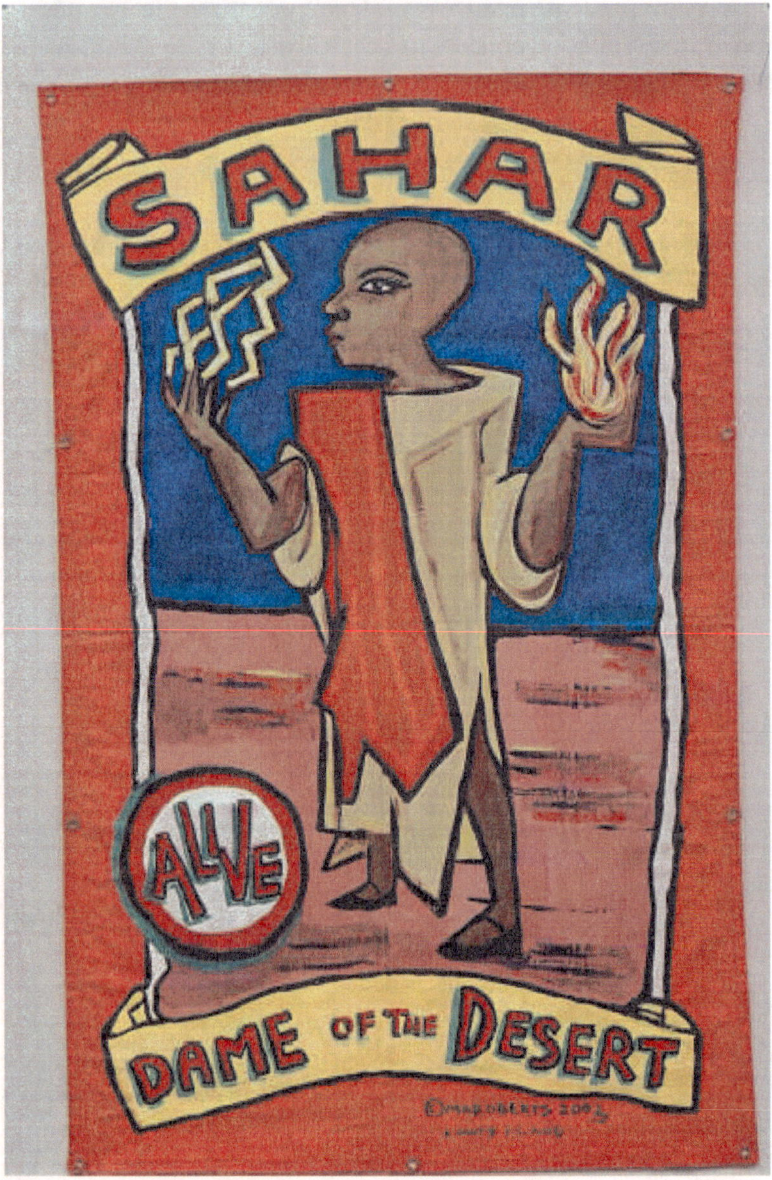
SAHAR
ALIVE
DAME OF THE DESERT

Reflection, the view from a distance, makes a liberal, a free relation with the world possible, one which is not determined by fear and worry. This liberal relationship makes beautiful appearance possible, play, which is not only possible, but also necessary in the face of an unbearable reality, which throws us into worry and fear. Therefore, the cultivation of beautiful appearance is not only the basis of human education, not only the basis of culture, but is culture itself.

Schiller's central problem is the relation between nature and freedom. How can freedom be real, and not only possible, within a nature which endangers and worries us? Nature itself cannot answer this question. If we regard ourselves as purely natural beings, then we never reach freedom. For this discovery, we don't need brain science, this was already clear to Kant and Schiller. If we regard ourselves as autonomous rational beings who act according to Kant's categorical imperative, or who can at least comprehend its incomprehensibility, then we find ourselves as free beings. How can both ways come together? How can we be free as natural beings?

I have already, with regard to Kant, hinted at the fact that beauty aims at a kind of negotiation, which wants to experience the play of cognitive powers as freedom.

Schiller transgresses Kant in this aspect. For Schiller, negotiation between nature and freedom is a universal demand, an unconditional imperative which succeeds through play in beauty.

> "Accordingly, as soon as reason issues the mandate, 'a humanity shall exist,' it proclaims at the same time the law, "there shall be a beauty.'" (Schiller, LETTERS ON THE AESTHETIC EDUCATION OF MAN)

Why shall there be a beauty? Why should form become a living form? Because we carry those two worlds within ourselves, the realm of nature and the realm of freedom; they express themselves in and through us. Thus, man can be truly human only if both, nature and freedom, sensuality and reason, are negotiated through play and in beauty.

Because beauty shall be, man becomes human in play. We are not to recognize beauty only by contemplation, but we are also called upon to realize it and to build our culture upon it.

However, a main place in which culture realizes this play is in the theater. Here, not only those themes come to performance which move our inner selves, but also those which force us to deal with them, as they constitute the essence of our being: love and hate, joy and sorrow, youth and old age, freedom and guilt, life and death. Here, pure nature does not offer orientation for action, no answer to the question: "What ought I to do?" Only in the way of dissociated contemplation and in the play which negotiates nature and freedom can we deal with those themes and can we approach them in the first place without drowning in their immediacy. In this sense, Schiller also takes up the Aristotelian moment of catharsis.

> "The depicting of suffering, in the shape of simple suffering, is never the end of art, but it is of the greatest importance as a means of attaining its end. The highest aim of art is to represent the super-sensuous, and this is effected in particular by tragic art, because it represents by sensible marks the moral man, maintaining himself in a state of passion, independently of the laws of nature. [...] Passion must be in play, that the reasonable being may be able to testify his independence and manifest himself in action."
> (Schiller, THE PATHETIC)

Schiller emphasizes over and over again that we must not be concerned in an immediate and existential way by the suffering which is staged before our eyes. If we are concerned in such a way, we are not free, according to Schiller, to establish a theoretical relationship with this suffering. The real death of the actor, the artiste or the knife thrower's assistant dissolves all distance, as it would concern us in an existential way. If the moment of existential concern does not offer any possibility for reflection, even less for aesthetic judgment, there must be one possibility to keep our distance from this deeply distressing event. Only on the level of contemplation, of regarding the suffering which does not immediately concern the subject – as it is set in scene in writing and drama as the imagination of foreign suffering –, a feeling of the sublime as aesthetic enjoyment becomes possible.

> "Therefore the pathetic is the first condition required most strictly in a tragic author, and he is allowed to carry his description of suffering as far as possible, without prejudice to the highest end of his art, that is, without moral freedom being oppressed by it. He must give in some sort to his hero, as to his reader, their full load of suffering, without which the question will always be put whether the resistance opposed to suffering is an act of the soul, something positive, or whether it is not rather a purely negative thing, a simple deficiency." (Schiller, THE PATHETIC)

If we accept that the performers should ritualize the dangers, then how much avoidance of real risk in a good knife throwing act is acceptable?

A knife landing two millimeters from a target girl is very "near death" expirience, two centimeters away excites the merely voyeuristic among the audience, but two meters away invites the ridicule.

What constitutes acceptable drama and how do we recognize it as such?

With regard to the artiste, or the knife thrower and his assistant, if we want to grant them this tragic role, this will mean that a knife thrower and an assistant who do not express that they risk injury

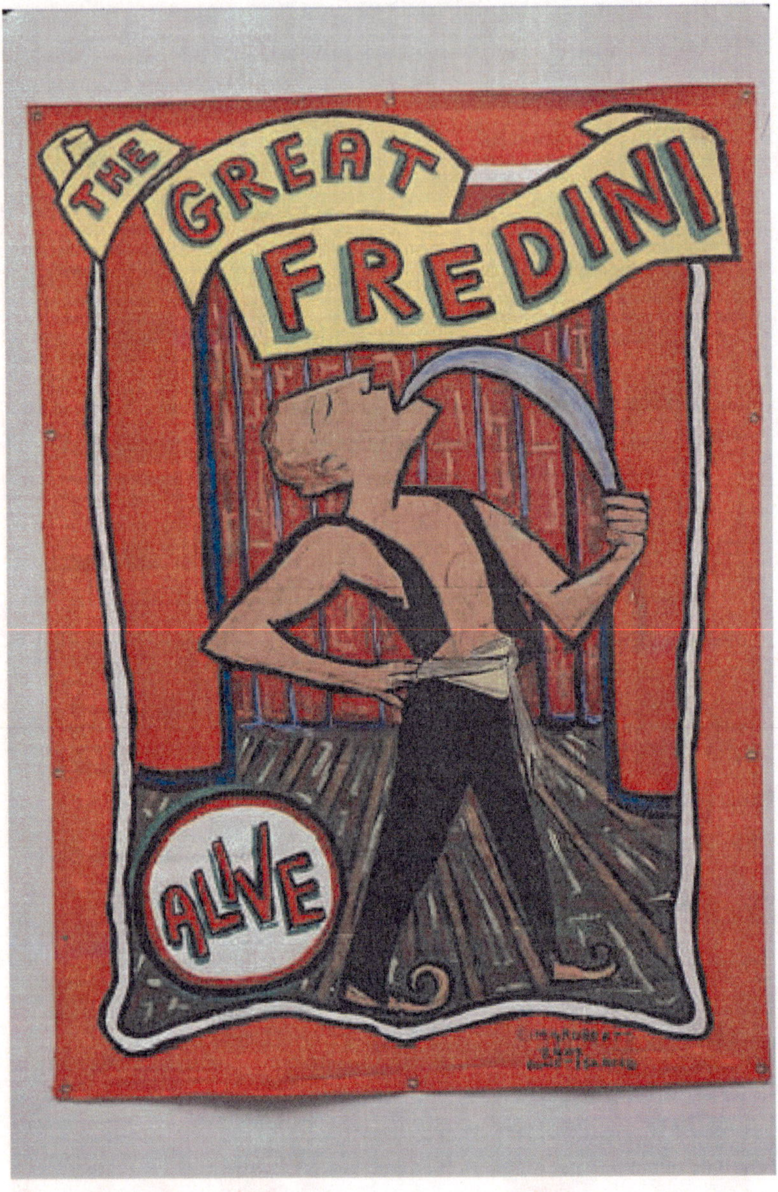
THE GREAT
FREDINI
ALIVE

the other or to be injured, and who act like machines, cannot be tragic heroes, just as the kind of knife thrower who attempts to stage a sado-masochist show with his assistant never can.

> "I imply by passion the affections of pleasure as well as the painful affections, and to represent passion only, without coupling with it the expression of the super-sensuous faculty which resists it, is to fall into what is properly called vulgarity; and the opposite is called nobility." (Schiller, THE PATHETIC)

If the movie "Girl on the Bridge" wants to imply that the knife thrower's assistant possibly becomes sexually aroused while knives are being thrown around her, this is everything but art! In this case, the audience would hardly have the impression that a knife throwing show could also be about the tragedy of life and the thought of freedom. It is another question whether everybody shouldn't have fun as well. There is no doubt that fun is an essential part of play and is also needed to make the contrasts of life. But art is not just about voluptuousness or fun, but about the seriousness of play.

On the other hand, it is also valid that for the actor, the artiste, or the knife thrower and his assistant, the representation of suffering, not the actual suffering, is important. If the audience becomes totally absorbed by the sensuous danger, the sense of the production will be missed.

> "But, on the other hand, real taste excludes all extreme affections, which only put sensuousness to the torture, without giving the mind any compensation. These affections oppress moral liberty by pain, as the others by voluptuousness; consequently they can excite aversion, and not the emotion that would alone be worthy of art. Art ought to charm the mind and give satisfaction to the feeling of moral freedom. This man who is a prey to his pain is to me simply a tortured animate being, and not a man tried by

suffering. For a moral resistance to painful affections is already required of man – a resistance which can alone allow the principle of moral freedom, the intelligence, to make itself known in it." (Schiller, THE PATHETIC)

If a knife throwing show is to be presented as an art, it is not a question of being the most dangerous show, but of being the most dramatic one.

For the actor, the knife thrower and his assistant, as for all artistes it counts to stage the drama of life. However, this neither happens in such a way that their play dissolves in the purely sensual, nor in fully leaving the sensual behind. What should entertain the audience is not mere danger or ability, but the staging of the dramaturgy of life in its wholeness.

Ultimately, for Schiller, art is about setting the audience into relation to the sublime, that is, to the idea of freedom. This sublime, however, shows itself in the dissociated contemplation of life with all its terror and suffering. In this contemplation, we recognize that we are more than merely sensuous beings and that our origin cannot be fully traced back to nature. This recognition is the origin of the pleasure we gain when watching staged suffering and the tragedy.

"If it is so, the poets and the artists are poor adepts in their art when they seek to reach the pathetic only by the sensuous force of affection and by representing suffering in the most vivid manner. They forget that suffering in itself can never be the last end of imitation, nor the immediate source of the pleasure we experience in tragedy. The pathetic only has aesthetic value in as far as it is sublime. Now, effects that only allow us to infer a purely sensuous cause, and that are founded only on the affection experienced by the faculty of sense, are never sublime, whatever energy they may display, for everything sublime proceeds exclusively from the reason." (Schiller, THE PATHETIC)

The figure or persona which originally achieves this reconciliation is the suffering or tragic hero. He is the one who takes upon himself the sufferings of life, ultimately not only to pass through them, but also to transgress them and to bring before our eyes the totality of life.

However, Schiller writes about the figure of the hero:

> "There is no merit in mastering the feelings which only lightly and transitorily skim over the surface of the soul. But to resist a tempest which stirs up the whole of sensuous nature, and to preserve in it the freedom of the soul, a faculty of resistance is required infinitely superior to the act of natural force. Accordingly it will not be possible to represent moral freedom, except by expressing passion, or suffering nature, with the greatest vividness; and the hero of tragedy must first have justified his claim to be a sensuous being before aspiring to our homage as a reasonable being, and making us believe in his strength of mind." (Schiller, THE PATHETIC)

Can we really grant the knife thrower this tragic role? In the case of the clown, we would probably have less reservation. Why is this so? Because the clown as a figure expresses a totality which the knife thrower as a single character lacks. The clown is not of this world. Even though he appears with his entourage, he alone transgresses the boundaries of the sensuous. He holds the world in his hands, as he keeps recreating it in ever new ways before our eyes. The clown unites all principles in himself: life and death, love and hate, joy and sorrow, the masculine and the feminine. He does not need the ferocity of lions or the tight rope, in whose depths death awaits him. His theatrical art is in the collapse of the worlds

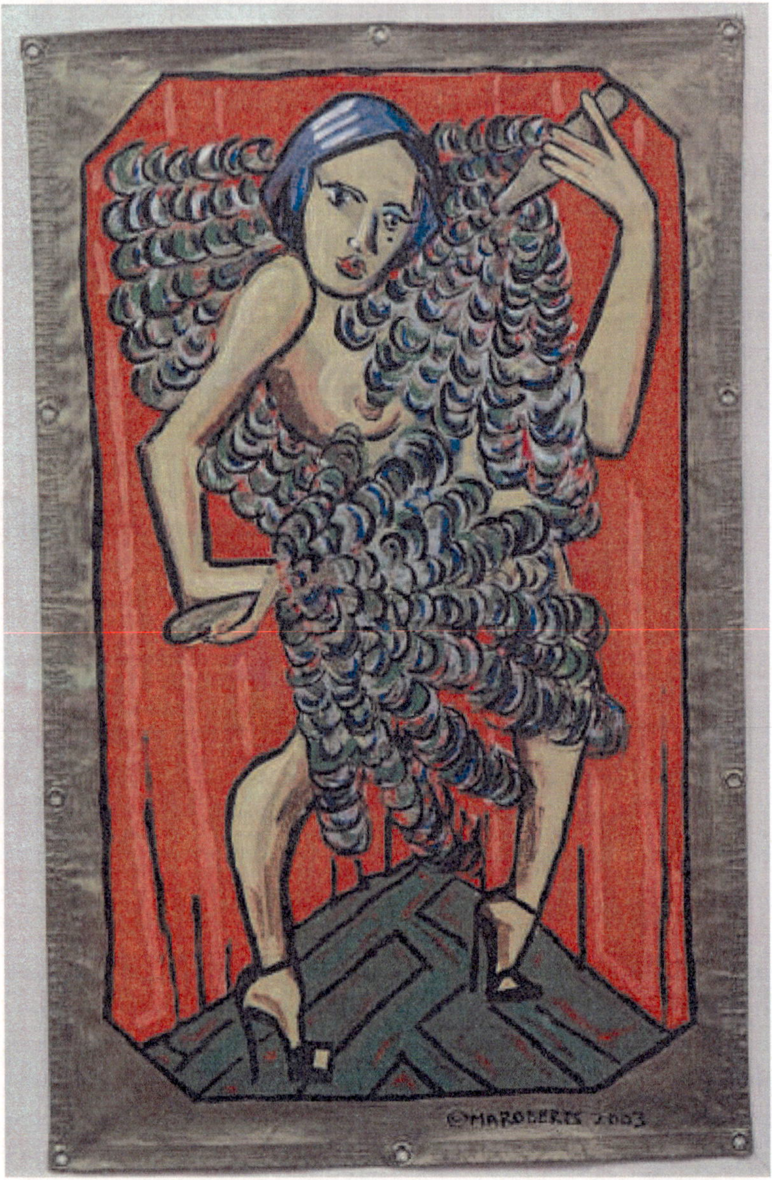

that he creates for us. To achieve the ability of the clown, the knife thrower needs a figure which brings himself and his action to totality: his assistant.

Only with the help of the assistant, the clown's countenance appears in the knife throwing act and only with the help of the assistant can the knife thrower succeed in telling a story: the story of life and death.

In examining the figure of the tragic hero, we will see that in fact the assistant, much more than the knife thrower himself, reminds of the hero.

Joseph Campbell, in his book THE HERO WITH A THOUSAND FACES, which first came out in 1949, examines most different myths for a common structure. Foregrounding especially the figure of the hero, he reaches the following conclusion:

> "The mythological hero, setting forth from his commonday hut or castle, is lured, carried away, or else voluntarily proceeds, to the threshold of adventure. There he encounters a shadow presence that guards the passage. The hero may defeat or conciliate and go alive into the kingdom of the dark (brother-battle, dragon battle; offering, charm), or be slain by the opponent and descent in death (dismemberment, crucifixion). Beyond the threshold, then, the hero journeys through of unfamiliar yet strangely intimate forces, some of which severely threaten him (tests), some of which give magical aid (helpers). When he arrives at the nadir of the mythological round, he undergoes a supreme ordeal and gains his reward. The triumph may be represented as the hero's sexual union with the goddess-mother of the world (sacred marriage), his recognition by the father-creator (father atonement), his own divinization (apotheosis), or again – if the powers have remained unfriendly to him – his theft of the boon he came to gain (bride-

theft, fire-theft); intrinsically it is an expansion of consciousness and therewith of being (illumination, transfiguration, freedom). The final work is that of the return. If the powers have blessed the hero, he now sets forth under their protection (emissary); if not, he flees and is pursued (transformation flight, obstacle flight). At the return threshold the transcendental powers must remain behind; the hero re-emerges from the kingdom of dread (return, resurrection). The boon that he brings restores the world (elixir)." (Campbell 1968, p. 245-246)

In THE WRITER'S JOURNEY: MYTHIC STRUCTURE FOR WRITERS, a book which, as the title already suggests, deals with the successful writing of movie shooting scripts and which was published in 1999, Christopher Vogler takes up Campbell's results and remarks:

> "All stories consist of a few common structural elements found universally in myths, fairy tales, dreams, and movies. They are known collectively as The Hero's Journey." (Vogler 1998, p. 1)

Vogler examines the different characters and figures of the myth, as the mentor, the shadow or the guard of thresholds. About the important figure of the hero, Vogler explains:

> "This is a critical moment in any story, an Ordeal in which the hero must die or appear to die so that she can be born again. It's a major source of magic in the heroic myth. The experiences of the preceding stages led us, the audience, to identify with the hero and her fate. What happens to the hero happens to us. We are encouraged to experience the brink-of-death moment with her. Our emotions are temporarily depressed so that they can be revived by the hero's return from death. The result of this revival is a felling of elation and exhilaration." (Vogler 1998, p. 22)

What Vogler touches upon here is, once again, the Aristotelian

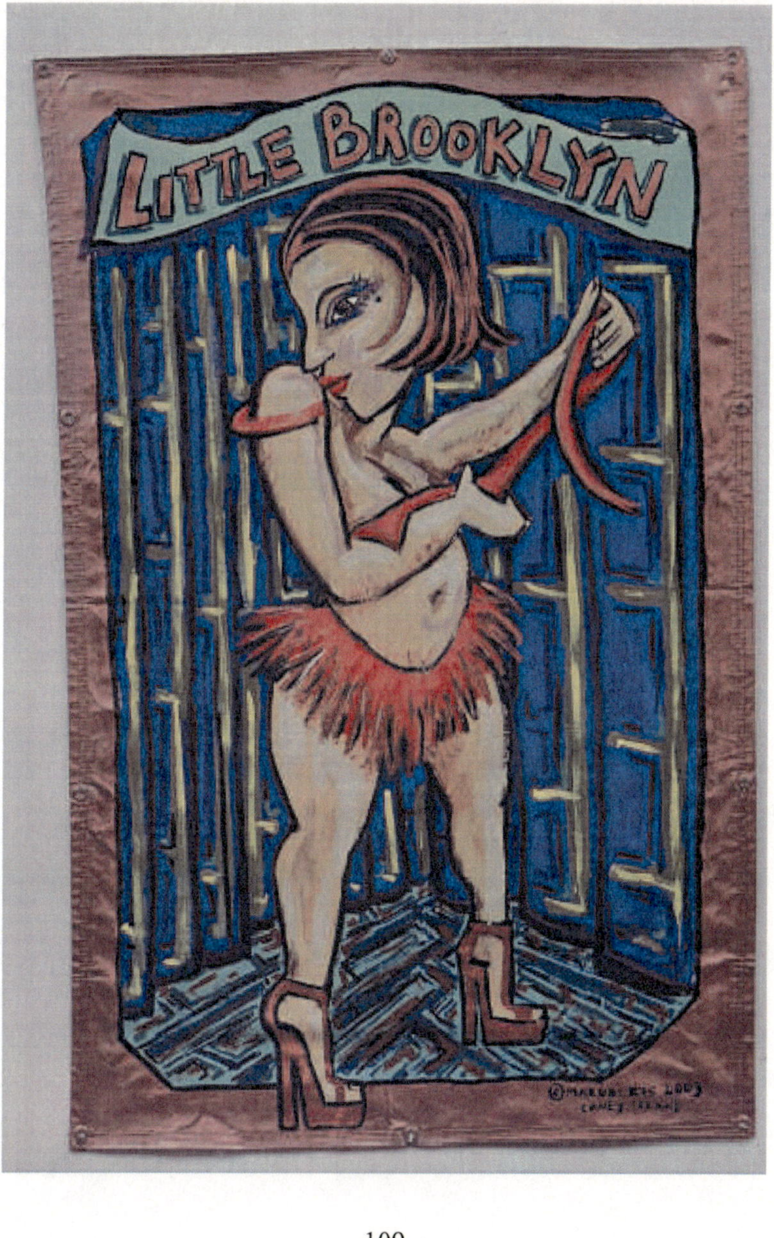
LITTLE BROOKLYN

element of catharsis.

So what exactly is the mythic or tragic hero's task? Stephan Grätzel makes a crucial point in his book DIE MASKEN DES DIONYSOS. Concerning the mythic hero, Grätzel writes:

> "The Hero is [...] not merely a muscleman, no superman, but a being willing to make sacrifices, a figure or person who stands in for others. The power of the hero is not high-handed, but arises from his service to others. The most important feature of the hero is his willingness to sacrifice his life, his devotion, and therefore something which aligns him with the figure of the shepherd. Due to this willingness to sacrifice and devotion, he becomes a deputy for the community which he saves. The message of salvation in the hero's story is indeed the savior of the whole of society and not merely of the hero himself. If the hero saves only himself, we have no heroic story, but a useless story; no story at all, strictly speaking. The hero serves society and assists it in the most important problem of all, that is, in the reconciliation of life and death" (Grätzel 2005, p. 138).

Thus, the myth is about the mystery of life and death, about the reconciliation of the living with the dead and the integration of death and the dead into life, which the hero achieves. The myth wants to offer an orientation concerning questions of gilt and right, which pose themselves to man as a being within a greater community. Thereby, it refers to the origin and searches the continuity of history and the connection of this origin with history. In this, the myth is concerned not about the fate of the individual, but about the fate of all, or, to speak once again with Christopher Vogler:

> "They [the myths and mystic stories, J. H.] deal with the childlike universal questions: Who am I? Where did I come from? Where will I go when I die? What is good and what is evil? What must

I do about it? What will tomorrow be like? Where did yesterday go? Is there anybody else out there?" (Vogler 1998, p. 11)

These childlike, original questions, these basic questions of being human are the big questions which trouble man in the works of Kant, the questions about the immortality of the soul, the possibility of man's freedom and the being of God. They are the reason why we are telling stories in the first place, why we act on the stage, indeed why we should act in the sense of theater as a form of art.

We see now from a philosophical perspective the high ambitions which are connected to the art of writing and telling stories, of acting and all other forms of art.

I now claim that the persona of the clown in the circus ring appears with these very ambitions. Whether the artiste who incorporates the mask or persona of the clown – be it the knife thrower, his assistant, the lion tamer, the tightrope walker, the magician or the juggler – are really able to live up to those expectations, is another question. It is crucial, however, that they confront these expectation and try to live up to them. Then, and only then, we can speak of art in the essential sense.

The knife thrower's assistant here achieves a special role: whatever she suffers, we suffer also; whatever happens to her happens to us. She suffers the fear of death, its unmediated presence in life, without actually experiencing death. Death is present in the knife thrower, but it can only be staged by the figure of the assistant, who represents mortality. She is the figure who makes us face mortality, who integrates death into life and simultaneously shows us ways to transgress death: in the dramaturgy of the play and of art. Here, the possibility opens up to integrate death into life without being engulfed by it. Only here, we succeed in playing with death and to deal with it.

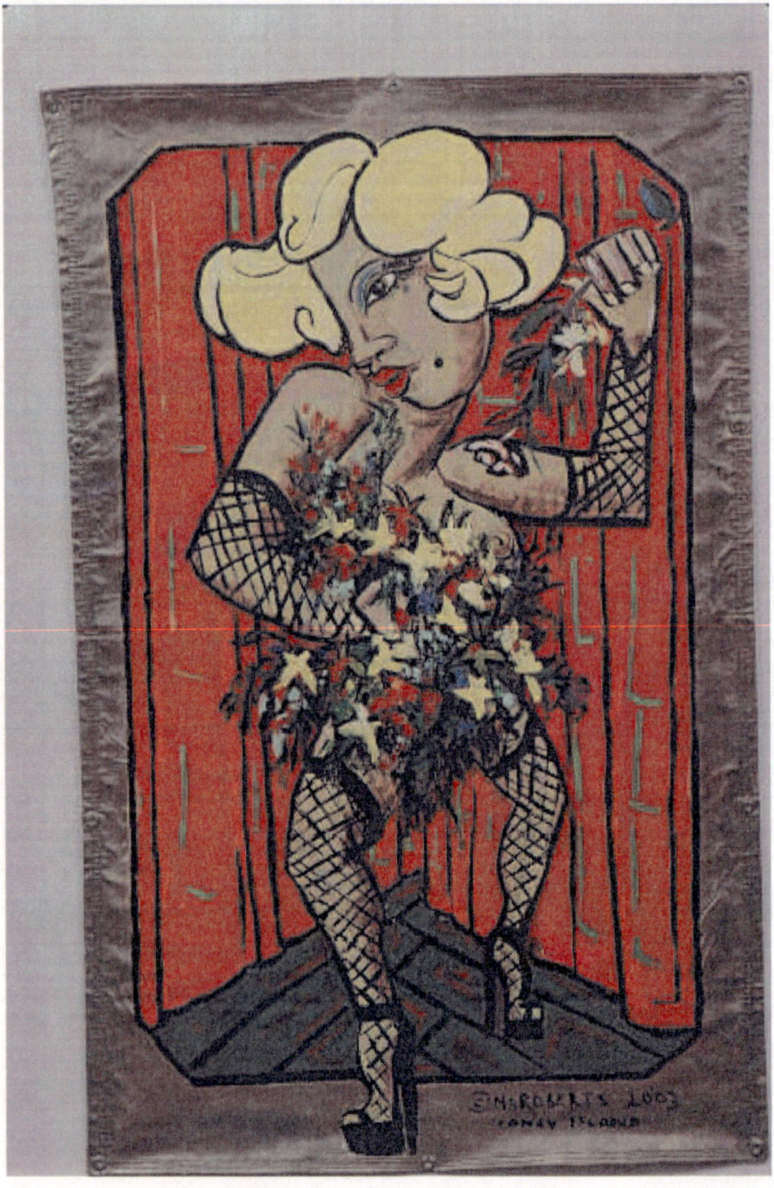

It is also interesting in this context to think about the meaning of the knife throwing show, and other circus acts as well, in terms of a cultic action. In the initiation rites of archaic cultures, we find the element to confront the initiate directly with death, which she or he seemingly suffers in the rite. In the rite, the initiate is brought into connection with the dead souls of his ancestors who guarantee the social order. She or he is taught obedience to tribal customs through fear and reverence for their superhuman authority. Those rites are a kind of atonement, which aims at purity. I can only hint at what Arnold van Gennep has described in his book Rites of Passage. It is crucial that the initiation rites also deal with the connection of life with death, its integration into life and, ultimately, with a form of purity. Yet, what is at stake here is purification from the guilt which inhabits human life: life always means to live on the cost of other life.

Thus, connected to life there is always guilt, a burden. Cult, myth and art bring a common theme to this burden of life. In taking it as a theme, however, they also open up a possibility to deal with this burden. What the cult initiates, the myth narrates and art presents, is life in its wholeness. Not a life beyond death, but life as a wholeness of life and death.

Obviously, what I could do in this context was only hinting at what a philosophy of the circus could be. At least one thing becomes clear: if circus really wants to be an art, it has to be more ambitious than simply wanting to represent technical mastery on the stage. One cannot live up to such ambitions by staging ever more colorful, avant-gardist and perfectionist shows. A knife thrower who only aims at presenting stunts which are as dangerous as possible merely limits himself and fails in telling a story which truly moves us.

I do believe that David holds those ambitions which link knife throwing with art, in regard to himself and his assistant. It has become clear to me through many talks with him that he wants more than to stage his own person and his abilities. In fact, I do believe that he tells a story in his show, which is about life and death, love and hate, joy and sorrow and which sets us into relation to the world in which man alone possesses infinity: the realm of ideas. What we make of it, is entirely up to us.

Literature

Campbell, Joseph: THE HERO WITH A THOUSAND FACES
2nd Edition, Princeton, New Jersey:
Princeton University Press, 1968.

Grätzel, Stephan: DIE MASKEN DES DIONYSOS
London: Turnshare, 2005

Kant, Immanuel KANTS WERKE
Akademie-Textausgabe
Berlin: de Gruyter, 1968 ff.

Schiller, Friedrich: SÄMTLICHE WERKE
3. Auflage, München: Carl Hanser, 1962.

Van Gennep, Arnold: THE RITES OF PASSAGE
Chicago: University of Chicago,
1960 (1908).

Vogler, Christopher: THE WRITER'S JOURNEY:
MYSTIC STRUCTURE FOR WRITERS
2nd Edition, Studio City, CA:
Michael Wiese Productions, 1998.

115

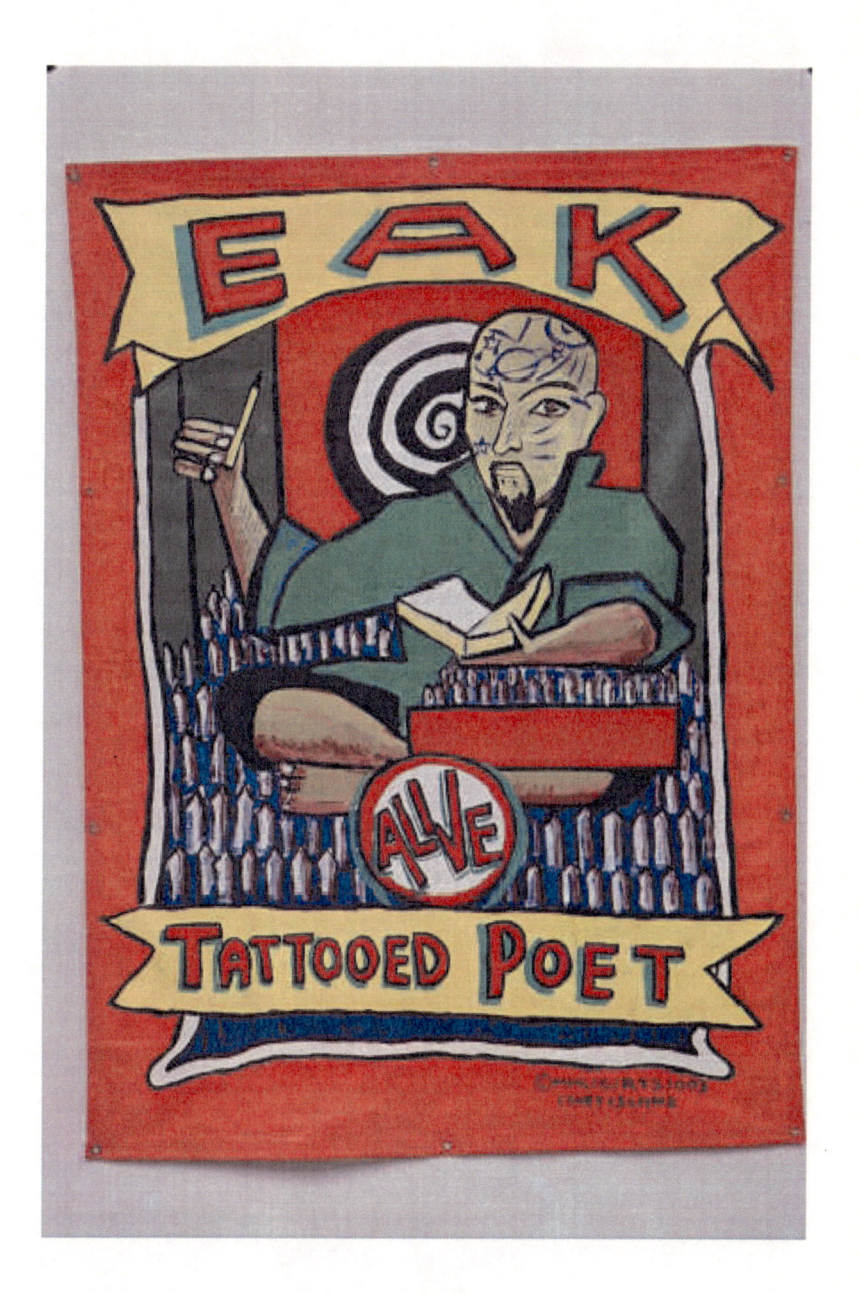

Sideshow Banners by Marie Roberts

p. 84 **SERPENTINA**, acrylic on canvas, 5' x 4', 2003, collection Stephanie Torres, NYC

p. 88 **THE AMAZING BLAZING TYLER FYRE**, acrylic on canvas, 7' x 5', 2002, collection Tyler Fyre, NYC

p. 93 **PAINPROOF (front)**, acrylic on canvas, 7' x 5', 2005, courtesy the artist

p. 94 **PAINPROOF (back)**, acrylic on canvas, 7' x 5', 2005, courtesy the artist

p. 98 **SAHAR**, acrylic on canvas, 6' x 4', 2003, courtesy the artist

p. 102 **THE GREAT FREDINI**, acrylic on canvas, 7' x 5', 2003, collection The Great Fredini, NYC

p. 106 **FANS**, acrylic on canvas, 6' x 4', 2003, collection D. Stern, AZ

p. 109 **LITTLE BROOKLYN**, acrylic on canvas, 6' x 4', 2003, courtesy the artist

p. 112 **FLOWERS**, acrylic on canvas, 6' x 4', 2003, collection D. Stern, AZ

p. 115 **EAK**, acrylic on canvas, 7' x 5', 2003, collection E Arrocha, NYC

all photographs by JAMES DEE, NYC

MARIE A ROBERTS

Marie Roberts earned her BA at Brooklyn College and her MFA at Queens College, CUNY. Artist in residence at Coney Island USA, Roberts has revived the century old tradition of banner painting in Coney Island.

Her large banner paintings are seen on the façade of Sideshows by the Seashore at Coney Island and the Annual Village Voice Siren Music Festival. Besides flying on the midway Roberts has exhibited in traditional gallery settings, most recently two of her banners were chosen for PROJECT DIVERSITY; one at Red Clay Arts@ Skylight Gallery in Bedford Stuyvesant and one at Rotunda Gallery in Brooklyn Heights.

She is represented in private and public collections, including the Metropolitan Transit Authority, NYC.

She is currently a Full Professor of Art at Fairleigh Dickinson University, Teaneck, NJ.

Roberts lives and works in the Coney Island/Gravesend area in the house her grandfather bought in 1919, where the ghosts of Dreamland still linger.

Marie Roberts & Tyler Fyre at Brooklyn Museum
Photo by Norman Blake

Marie Roberts
Photo by Frank Goldblatt

**Marie Roberts
and
Chris McDaniel**
Photo by Norman Blake

**Marie Roberts
and
Throwdini**
Photo by Barbara Adamovich

Marie Roberts
Photo by markmurraystudio.com

Marie Roberts

Autobiographical notes about
The Great Throwdini

The introductory comments to the audience in my cabaret act goes something like this, "Good evening ladies and gentlemen, my real name is The Rev. Dr. David Adamovich; retired professor with a doctorate in exercise physiology, paramedic, pool hall owner, professionally trained chef, ordained minister of the gospel AND in my spare time, I throw knives." So there you go, a very brief outline and only a hand full of hats I wear and have worn in real life.

My high school career was far from stellar. One teacher told my parents I was not college material. Another said not to worry; he's a late bloomer. The latter was right on the money. Despite going to undergraduate school with a major in physical education I had no desire to actually teach physical education, in other words to be a "gym teacher."

I took physical education because I was a good gymnast in high school. In fact my team, though underdogs, won the New York City Championships. We were a team that didn't even have uniforms as compared to other high school teams that looked like Olympic athletes. I was an ace student in anatomy and took a natural liking toward exercise physiology — the study of what happens to the body as a result of exercise. My university was just beginning a master's degree program in exercise physiology the semester following my undergraduate studies. The decision was an

Throwdini on TV show Blind Date

easy one — stay in school and get a graduate degree instead of finding a teaching job. I applied for and was granted a teaching fellowship. Thus, I would teach undergraduate classes in return for a tuition free graduate education. To help support married life I worked part time at a hospital in Brooklyn, NY in the Department of Rehabilitation Medicine, conducting exercise stress tests and training patients with cardiovascular and pulmonary diseases.

As I was finishing my master's degree at Long Island University and presenting my thesis about interval training in people with cardiovascular and pulmonary disease I was attracted to a doctoral program in exercise physiology at Teachers College of Columbia University, one of the top three graduate schools in the country. I

> **INTERNATIONAL KNIFE THROWERS HALL OF FAME**
>
> INDUCTS
>
> DR. DAVID ADAMOVICH
> "THE GREAT THROWDINI"
>
> AS
>
> **2003 OUTSTANDING ACHIEVEMENT IN THE IMPALEMENT ARTS AWARD**
>
> THE IKTHOF PROUDLY RECORDS THE INDUCTEE INTO THE CATEGORY MENTIONED ABOVE FOR THE YEAR 2003. THIS IS THE ULTIMATE RECOGNITION BY YOUR PEERS IN KNIFE THROWING, AND ALL PRIMARY AND SECONDARY INFORMATION IS RECORDED AT THE HALL OF FAME HEADQUARTERS IN AUSTIN, TEXAS, USA PRESENTED THIS ELEVENTH DAY OF OCTOBER TWO THOUSAND AND THREE
>
> DR. MICHAEL J. BAINTON – DIRECTOR
> INTERNATIONAL KNIFE THROWERS HALL OF FAME ASSOCIATION

received a second master's degree and a doctorate in the next three years. My dissertation was on systolic time intervals, i.e., the contractile times of the left ventricle under a variety of rest and exercise conditions in healthy sedentary, athletes, and individuals who've suffered heart attacks. At that time I was off to the real world as a cardiovascular exercise physiologist at a big county hospital. I started off in the Department of Rehabilitation Medicine and quickly moved to Cardiology. It was then that I fully mastered the art and science of electrocardiography and exercise testing, conducting research and developing treadmill tests to aid in the discharge of patients. I was asked to teach electrocardiography to graduate exercise physiology students at Adelphi University in Garden City, NY. I would continue on that path as an adjunct professor and ultimately full time professor over the next eighteen years.

Somewhere along the way I also took on an adjunct position at Queens College, NY. My students were so fascinated with the topic that they wanted my notes. I told them I didn't use notes to teach, it was all in my head! So I took on the task of writing down the notes and 425 pages later I published what became the gold standard of electrocardiography teaching text books within my field, THE HEART: FUNDAMENTALS OF ELECTROCARDIO-GRAPHY, EXERCISE PHYSIOLOGY

Maximum Risk, acrylic on canvas, 6' x 4' 2003
by Marie Roberts

AND STRESS TESTING. In the evenings after teaching I would sneak off to the billiard hall and work as "house man" from ten PM through three AM the next morning. I loved to play pool and was fairly good at it. Working in the pool hall gave me the time to relax from my professional world and de-velop my game further. In addition, I had the opportunity to learn about the business end of the industry. Ultimately, it would open the door to knife throwing, something I hadn't even heard about until the age of fifty.

Jenn

After four years at the hospital, I was recruited by a university to direct their fitness program and to perform cardiac stress tests on their members. I did this for a number of years as well as work privately with cardiologists in their offices performing cardiac stress tests while they conducted their practice seeing patients. After a number of years doing this I finally took a full time job as director of the graduate exercise physiology program at Long Island University, my alma mater. After nearly five years at the university I had to make a decision, apply for tenure or leave to take a full time position as executive vice president in an emergency medicine management company. I opted to leave academia and once again join the real world. It was fine and lasted about four years until the president decided to sell the company. Somewhere in all this I decided to study religion and become a minister. It was done and over. I was ordained and suddenly found myself doing weddings, funerals and baptisms. The entire ministerial aspect of my life is worthy of a book by itself. You wouldn't believe what can go wrong during a wedding

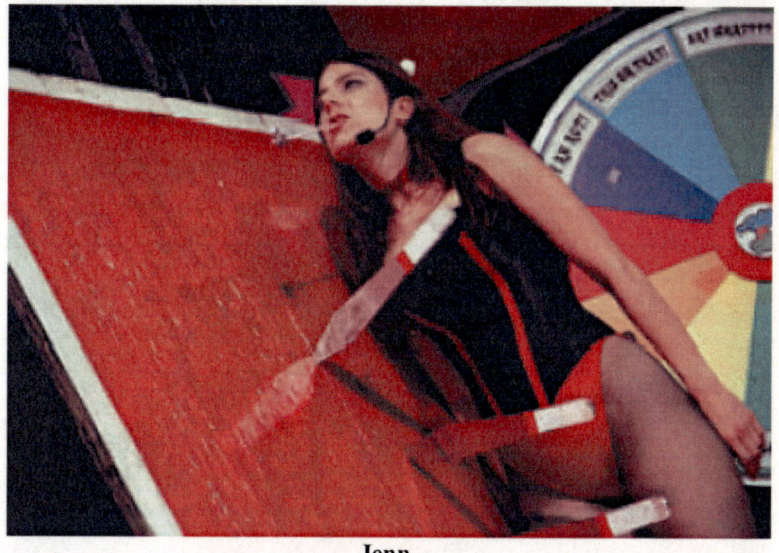

Jenn
Photo by Laure Leber

ceremony. As the saying goes, "If anything can go wrong, it will," and it invariably does. But since I never talk about religion or politics I won't go further with that other than to say the ministry led me to become a Chaplain for the volunteer fire service. That led me to becoming an emergency medical technician and ultimately a paramedic. That, of course, gave me the opportunity to save the life of a woman who went into cardiac arrest (using a defibrillator), who shortly thereafter died at the hospital, was asked by her family to administer final prayers and then ultimately preside over her funeral. Now wasn't that a fateful day to ride the ambulance!

OK, enough about religion and being a paramedic and back to emergency medicine management. I found myself out of work with

Ula

a wall full of degrees and professional diplomas, a thick resume with scientific research and a textbook under my belt, I thought I would be a great find for prospective employers. Just the opposite. It was virtually impossible for a 50-year-old with a strong background to compete with new graduates. I suppose

128

they figured I was untouchable and didn't even offer me a position even though I was the one who perfectly fit their want ads. So what else was I to do? I looked back upon my younger days and turned to a previous love — billiards. I bought a pool hall.

After just one year working the hall three fourteen-hour days per week (I had a manager that worked the other four) I was getting

Ula
Photo by Laure Leber

pretty good at my pool game. I had a continuous run in straight pool of 62. Not bad, but not professional either. One day one of my customers, Joe Torraca, came in and while playing pool with me pulled a small throwing knife out of his pocket. He asked me if I'd ever thrown one. Never even considered it, I told him. So we went outside and he showed me how to throw it at a tree. I stuck it

Ula and Throwdini
Photos by Barbara Adamovich

131

132

133

perfectly on my first attempt. I said in all modesty, "I can do that, it's easy." In the next three months the fever of throwing was going through the roof. I bought some throwing knives and began searching the Internet for other knife throwers. Enter Harry Munroe, aka Der Werfer. He lived just 3 hours drive from me and I was off to throw

Katya and Throwdini

with a real knife thrower. Harry was the New England Champion and showed me different throws from different distances I never tried before. I asked him about competition throwing and he said, "If you want to be one of the big boys you have to throw with the big boys." He was referring to the World Championship sponsored by the IKTA, International Knife Throwing Alliance, held annually in Las Vegas, NV.

Six months later my wife and I were on a plane to the championships. It was a two-day elimination event in which each thrower had to put five knives into a target from five different

distances, throwing one half, one, one and one half, two and two and one half spins of the knife. At the end of the first day I was second in the elimination down to six who would go into the finals. I was one point away from the previous world record and just behind the previous world champion. All this happened within nine months of me throwing my first knife at the age of fifty. It was a lot of pressure and the next day it caught up. I failed to stick a few knives and my

Katya and Throwdini

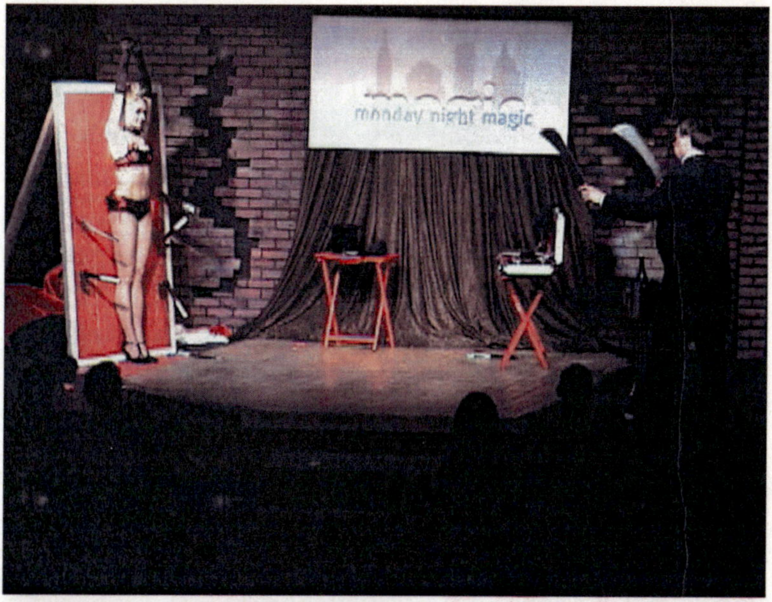
monday night magic

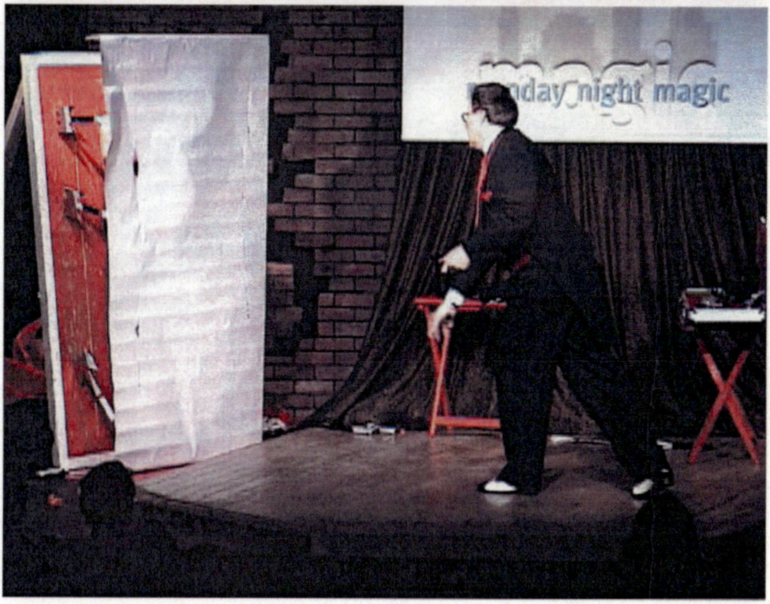
magic
monday night magic

score brought me out of the top three. But the man running the contest, Bob "Master of the Blade" Karp, told everyone to watch me carefully. I was the "smoothest" knife thrower he had ever seen. Some of the other competitors were throwing perhaps twenty years. And there I was, my first tournament after nine months of throwing and already a force to contend with.

In my last year of competition I set out to produce a one-hour video/DVD on knife throwing. It came after visiting a champion knife thrower from San Diego, Carl Geddes. He and I were analyzing each other's throwing style when the idea hit me like a ton of bricks. The idea of analyzing and teaching knife throwing needed to be documented in video form. My "throw-and-peel" method worked good for me and I felt the need to share it with others. After all, eighteen years as a professor, teaching was ingrained in me. At the time only one other contemporary video on knife throwing, produced by John Bailey from Florida, existed. John and I spoke about my idea of microanalyzing knife throwing and we both knew there was more to do — a void to be filled.

It was a monumental task being self-produced, self-starred, self-everything. It was a labor of love in which hours of taping would eventually make minutes of final product. This was the first instructional video to demonstrate a thrown knife from five different angles in real time, slow motion and frame-by-frame analysis. It documented just how the knife leaves the hand and how it spins toward the target. I further demonstrated each of the existing competition formats: the AKTA (American Knife Throwers Alliance and it's sister PKT, Pacific Knife Throwers), the IKTA (International Knife Throwing Alliance), and WFKT (World Federation of Knife Throwers). In each case I put all thrown knives into an 8 inch ring at every distance from one half spin at eight feet to two and one half spins at 21 feet without a miss or out-take. Now in its second edition,

Allison
Photo by Nikolai Komissarov

Fundamentals of Knife, Tomahawk and Axe Throwing with an Introduction to the Impalement Arts, includes my impalement arts promo with clips from different TV and stage performances. I'm very proud of the project and believe it's among the best, if not the very best, production on knife throwing ever undertaken.

Over the next four years of competition throwing I won both national and world championship titles. I had my fill of competition throwing and realized I was destined to take on the ultimate challenge, the impalement arts — throwing knives around a human assistant. Enter Chris McDaniel. Chris was a world champion trick roper and performer that lives about one hour from me. He saw an article about me in a variety arts magazine, TIME OUT NY, and called saying he'd like to get together as he'd like to add some knife throwing to his stage show. Chris asked if I was interested in performing versus being a competition thrower. I said no, I was just a competition thrower. He showed me some videotape of professional knife throwers performing in the '50s through the '70s.

There were very few artists left here in the United States as the variety arts of that type were pretty much on the decline and the previous guys were dying off or retiring. I was so excited about what I saw on those tapes, I kept saying, "I could do that. I could do that." And so I did. Just two weeks later I sent Chris a videotape of me reproducing all the stunts performed by the masters of professional knife throwing. He was duly impressed and invited me to watch him perform a mini version of his One-Man Wild West Show at an upcoming performance of Monday Night Magic. My wife and I went and I knew right then and there I wanted to perform.

For the next year I worked on my routine, perfecting an act with nothing more than a mannequin and a knife board. The Wheel of Death was just a dream. Over time, Chris worked with me choreographing every step and script of the act. He really did a great job in turning a

Allison
Photo by Nikolai Kamissarov

knife thrower into a performer using knives to entertain the audience. There is a big difference between the two. A lot of people can throw knives but there's a big expanse between sticking a knife and turning it into a 20-minute cabaret act that entertains a paying audience. Chris did that for me. I shall always be grateful. In addition I have befriended two other associates of Chris's who've influenced me greatly — Simon Lovell and Todd Robbins. Simon and Todd are recognized internationally for their particular expertise. Simon is a sleight-of-hand card magician

Throwdini and Ula
Photo by Dale Rio

and comedian and Todd is THE Modern Master of the Sideshow. All three of them, Chris, Simon and Todd are constantly tweaking the act; stand here…say this…say that…try this…etc. It amazes me with what they see and are able to suggest in making a good stunt a great stunt. I suppose that's what makes them the great performers they are.

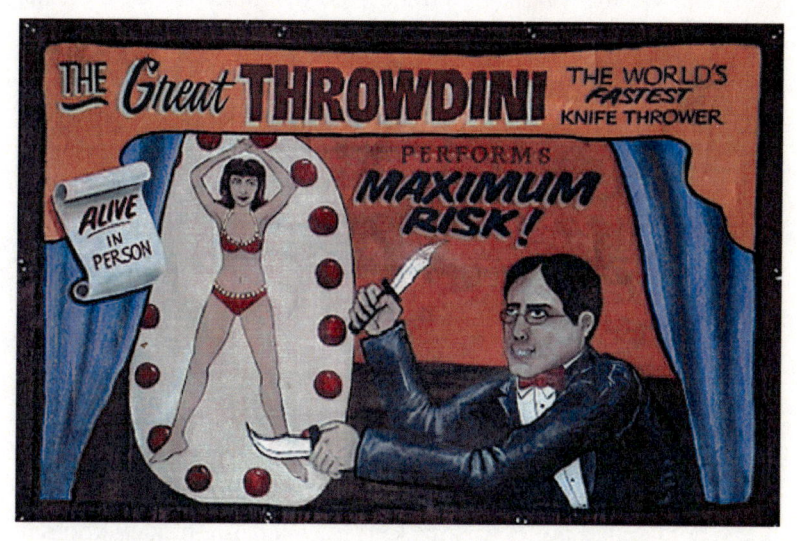

Throwdini in the play Big Top at the Red Room, NYC

I needed a name for my act. I was a fan of the French movie, Girl on the Bridge; a movie about a burnt-out knife thrower who seeks assistants on bridges as he sees destitute girls about to commit suicide. While knife thrower Gabor hustles himself into a show he wasn't booked his assistant, Adele, is off in a corner flirting with a masked contortionist. The manager asks Gabor what's special or different about his act. Gabor peeks toward Adele and sees the masked contortionist. He says, "I throw blind, maximum risk." So there you have it, the birth of MAXIMUM RISK. I can't recommend this movie enough. It came out in 2000 and starred Daniel Auteuil and Vanessa Paradis. It was shot in black and white, spoken in French and has English subtitles. See it. You won't be sorry.

I visited Larry Cisewski, a professional thrower from the west coast. I wanted to learn what I could from a professional impalement artist. Larry showed me some cool stuff but more importantly gave me the confidence I needed to take my act to the next level. He simply said I was a great thrower and could do anything I wanted. That's all I needed to hear. My future was carved out for me right then and there. I subsequently got to throw with two other professionals, Dick Haines (The Dean of Knife Throwing) and Kenny Pierce (Che Che Whitecloud). From each I learned something new and something different. Most importantly I gathered confidence. All I needed was an assistant, a partner who trusted me and who would let an aspiring impalement artist throw knives at, or as I prefer to say, around. A great professional knife thrower from the past, Frank Dean, once said, "Never throw at a human target — throw around it. They last longer that way." Although I've never hit one of my assistants I must admit there has been a few mishaps over the thousands of knives thrown in both rehearsal and during live performances due to bounced or badly thrown knives. There are hidden knots in the wood that just spit the knives right back.

Speaking of assistants, most knife throwing acts developed as husband and wife teams. Where one goes the other goes, and they move through married life and show business together. My wife Barbara, on the other hand, has no interest in being my assistant. She's always preferred watching the knives from the thrower's point of view rather than the assistant's. An accom-plished knife thrower in her own right, Barbara took first place in the Women's Nationals in her first year of throwing, but dropped it quickly thereafter not having an interest to continue. She helped me rework some old stunts and even develop a new one, the "knife catch." One day I

Ula

Photo by Dale Rio

had a crazy idea that I could catch a knife thrown toward me while standing at the board. I asked her to throw some knives around me and without telling her what I would do I suddenly reached up and snatched the knife in flight. It's dangerous and crazy. Besides the risk of impaling my hand there's the possibility of a bad grab that deflects right into my face. None-the-less, I do it and have only allowed four people to be my thrower: Barbara, Chris McDaniel, Dick Haines and Harry Munroe. Maybe some day with the right assistant I could add it to my act.

Speaking of crazy stunts there is another one I developed with Harry (Der Werfer) Munroe using his wife Joan as our target girl. Joan and I were performing for the Bindlestiff Family Cirkus at Variety Palace in Times Square, New York. I announced to the audience there was another thrower in the audience and invited him down on stage to perform something never done before…the Double Ladder of Death. Since it was the first time we were attempting it we kept the pace only moderately fast, throwing about one knife per second each. The stunt involved each of us, the two throwers, throwing knives at the same pace but alternating our throws so that one knife would hit the board every half second. It sounded like a machine gun as we threw a total of 16 knives crisscrossing Joan. Harry and I threw to the opposite side of her body from where we were standing — thus the possibility of the knives colliding in the air. We did it a total of three times sticking every knife only once. It's a dangerous and fast stunt in which the opportunity for error to creep in is quite easy. On one occasion Harry missed the board on a wide throw and I missed impaling Joan's arm by less than an inch. I repeat, it's a dangerous stunt that involves precision timing and a fearless assistant. Target Girl Joan knew we could repeat it and do it

Jenn and Throwdini
Photo by Laure Leber

even faster. We eventually did. One day about a year later we threw sixteen knives across Joan with each of us throwing at 0.75 seconds/knife. The knives sounded like a machine gun as they impaled the board at an astonishing rate of 0.375 seconds apart, literally three per second.

Another stunt I created, along with the knife-catch, is the impalement of a chosen card from a deck of cards sprung in front of

Ula

the impalement board by my assistant. The timing is critical, the effect is phenomenal and a great finale to MAXIMUM RISK. Early on in the act I invite an audience volunteer on stage, my assistant blindfolds him and we pop balloons he holds under his arms and between his legs. Blindfolded, he thinks I'm throwing at the balloons. I throw away from his body and my assistant breaks the balloons with a pin. Before hooding him I ask him to randomly pick a card from a deck of cards. Making no attempt to identify the card I tell

Photo by clycreation.com

him we'll get back to that later on. And so we do, at the finale, just as he thinks I forgot all about him. He tells me the card, my assistant springs the cards in the air and I impale the chosen card to the board. Magicians are always finding selected cards, but impaling it in mid-air is a whole new ball game. I owe the development of this stunt to Francis Menotti, a magician from Pennsylvania, who allowed me to trash over a dozen decks of his cards in developing the technique necessary to perform the stunt. In addition, I use a beautiful 14 inch custom Bowie knife made for me by Joe "Brokenfeather" Darrah.

Back to my lovely and daring assistants — sine qua non — without which there'd be no act! All my assistants, perhaps six over the past three years of performing professionally, have been girls with careers of their own, mostly show business, that would very often conflict with my bookings as they may have their own bookings or jobs to deal with. Thus, the constant search for a partner that will always be available and willing to give up an appointment or job to be my assistant when I need her. On several occasions I've had to cancel or decline a gig because of not having an assistant. On the other hand, one girl actually dropped everything within one day and decided, like me, there was nothing more important than running away and joining the circus. We did. That story comes in a little later.

Although some venues just love my act it's difficult to book a knife show here in the United States. The atmosphere post September 11, 2001 has made any kind of "weapon" or perceived weapon politically incorrect. Variety artist's that use guns and/or knives are still having a difficult time four years later. I clearly recall being contacted by someone for a TV shoot. We discussed what I would do with my assistant and with the person that was being surprised by the throwing as part of the plot for the show. I got there, threw a few knives around my assistant and saw someone in the background feverishly making phone calls on her cell phone. A moment later I was told, "No more knives." From New York, one of the production assistants was on the phone with her lawyer back in Los Angeles. When they found out I was actually throwing REAL knives they freaked. What were they thinking when they booked me? Did they still think they would come from the back of the board? Oh well, that shoot was history real fast. Stated another way, I went from hero to zero in the blink of an eye.

New York's Longest Running Off-Broadway Magic Show

"New York's Best Magical Venue" - *TimeOut NY*
"Best of Manhattan" Award - *The New York Press*

PRODUCED BY MAGICAL NIGHTS INC

monday night magic

www.mondaynightmagic.com

Appearing Every Monday at 8:00 pm
The SoHo Playhouse
15 Vandam Street, NYC

(1 block north of Spring Street ...
... just west of 6th Avenue)
212.615.6432

Each and every week, a different show,
featuring the best magicians in the world.

Besides performing regularly on Monday Night Magic there's the occasional TV shoot, short film, and one of my favorites, the Side Show Circus at Coney Island, NY. It's a part of history to perform at Coney Island. Chris McDaniel and I created our own production, The Nuevo Variety Circus and Wild West Show. We usually include my assistant doing her own act, either a bed-of-swords or contortion act, a sword-swallower fire-eater, a juggler and aerialist. It's great for Coney Island and we get some of our best crowds, usually college age that have had a few drinks in them. They go nuts with every knife and with every stunt. My two favorite TV show performances were for Good Morning America with Charlie Gibson, Diane Sawyer and Tony Perkins in which we recreated the famous stunt in which

Astrid
Photo by T<small>HE</small> C<small>OUNCIL</small>

Ed Ames threw an axe into the crotch of a drawn figure on the Johnny Carson Show, and the Brini Maxwell Show in which I threw knives around an attractive six-foot blonde that was a man in disguise.

Most recently I had the immense pleasure of "running away and joining the circus" at the ripe old age of fifty seven! Literally speaking,

Astrid
Photo by THE COUNCIL

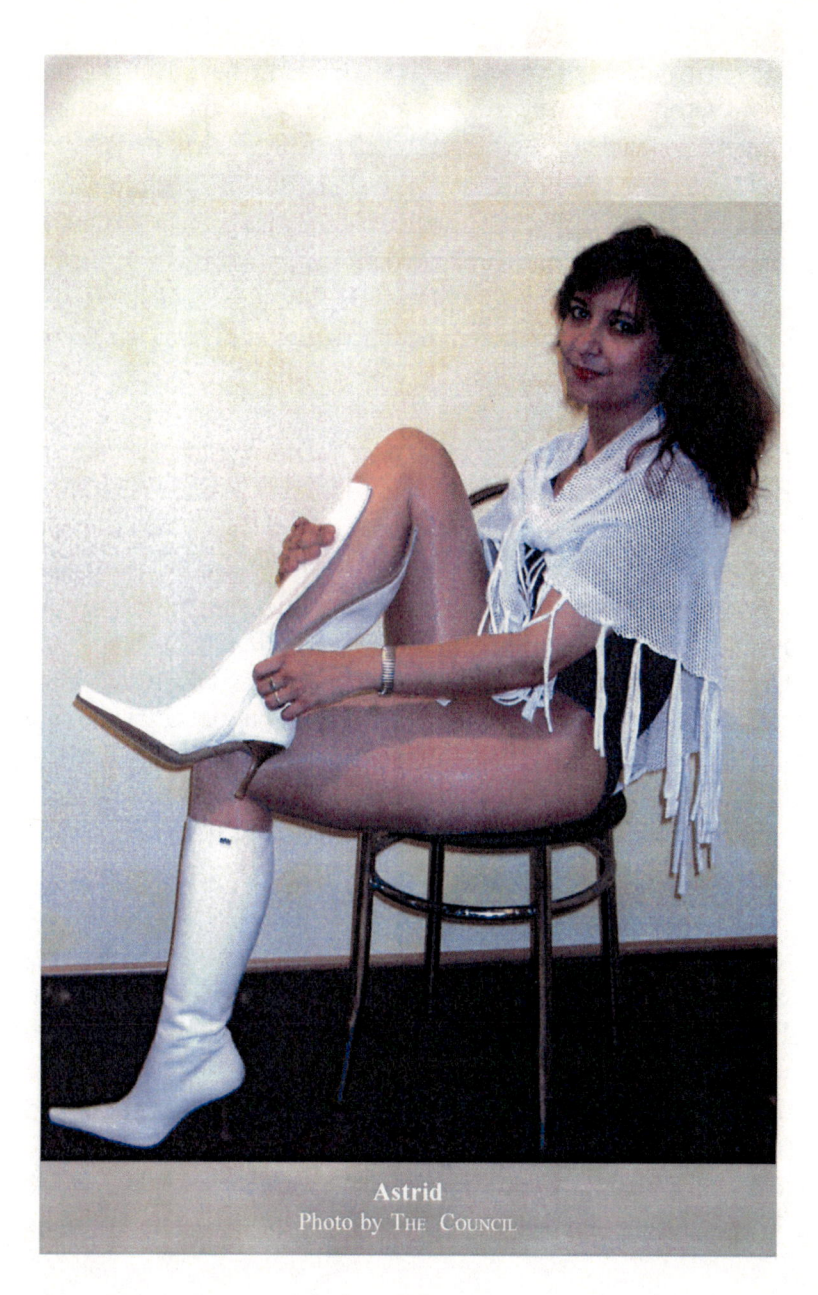

it saved my life. Prior to going on tour I decided to have a full physical exam to be sure I was in good shape to be on the road. It was discovered that I had prostate cancer. I had no signs nor symptoms and it was discovered in a routine blood test. All the possibilities were explored and my eldest daughter, Tara, a surgeon in Manhattan insisted I have the entire prostate removed by a surgeon trained in oncology at Sloan Kettering Memorial Hospital. I took her advice despite my wish to have nothing stand in the way of going on tour, in particular a lengthy recovery. So with less than two months before leaving I had a difficult six-hour operation to remove the cancer. Pathology showed it was at the margins of the prostate capsule and imminently due to spread. It was caught just in time. Anyway, I survived the operation but had a very difficult recovery as it had irritated three herniated discs in my lower back. For nearly one month I was bedridden and in crippling pain. I got over it and with just two weeks to go I had to get on my feet and leave for New Orleans. I practiced daily with whatever energy I could muster. Each day my throwing got noticeably better and the pre-operation thrower hidden within was breaking through. As the saying goes, "It's just like riding a bike." You just get on and go once you know how.

My assistant, Target Girl Ekaterina (Katya), and I were going on a two and a half month tour of southern United States with Stars of the World Famous Moscow State Circus. Two days before we were to leave she got news that her father passed away in Russia. She was off to be with the family and I was without an assistant. Fortunately a new partner, Target Girl Miss Allison (by utter coincidence happened to have attended high school with my younger daughter Tracy), that I had been teaching the act was more than anxious to fill in. I bought a motor home, had a wonderful going away party by family and friends, and we were off to join the circus. Although scheduled to be on the road for two and a half months touring the southern states, including a week in Alaska, we managed to get in 6 shows in New Orleans and got blasted out of town by the rapidly arriving storm Ivan. Just two days after our speedy departure from New Orleans, the main Interstate highway between Louisiana and Florida was washed away by storm floods. We got out of there just in time and headed back to New York. The tour did finish but

Ula and Throwdini

several of the venues were cancelled and it appears the best thing we did was head home in one piece. Would I run away with the circus again? You can bet on it. For now my immediate goals are to get booked in Las Vegas, the entertainment capital of the world. You bet your butt!

As fate would have it my relationship with Monday Night Magic came to a fork in the road. MNM decided to move to a mid-town theatre thus leaving Monday nights open at the SoHo Playhouse, NYC. This opened the door to produce my own show, MAXIMUM RISK — World Champions on the Edge!^{sm} starring The Great Throwdini, Chris McDaniel and Ekaterina, and to kick it off as an Off-Broadway production. The timing was just right and the opportunity was taken. The show is directed by none other than Simon Lovell, at this time star of his own Off-Broadway one-man show Strange and Unusual Hobbies, playing at the Huron Club, NYC, and written by Chris McDaniel and Simon Lovell. We're due to open June 6, 2005 at the SoHo Playhouse in NYC. Each show will feature a guest variety artiste as well as an attempt to either break or create a new world record. I, for example, intend to kick-off the premiere show by throwing 120 plus knives around my assistant in less than one minute! (In fact, this is less than my personal best to date, 144 knives in 60 seconds flat). But it's always good to hold back just a little with room to break my own record in future shows. Let's just keep that our dirty little secret, eh mate!

Last but not least I should add that some day you might run into another guy that looks just like me. My parents, Adam and Linda, hit the birth jackpot with an event that occurs four times in a thousand, i.e., identical twins. My brother Daniel got the jump on me by five minutes. (I was a big surprise back then, as expectant mothers didn't routinely get sonograms.) As the story goes, "Doctor, wait, there's another one." Daniel Adamovich, Ph.D., is alive and well and doesn't throw knives. He was an aeronautical engineer, flew jets in the US Air Force and now owns a computer store. Maybe I'll send him a set of throwing knives.

Poster created by Jim Glaub, sohoplayhouse.com
Photo by clycreation.com

Fellow Performers
Who've Influenced Throwdini

Chris McDaniel
chrismcdaniel.net

Michael Chaut
mondaynightmagic.com

Jamy Ian Swiss
jamyianswiss.com
Photo by Virginia Lee Hunter

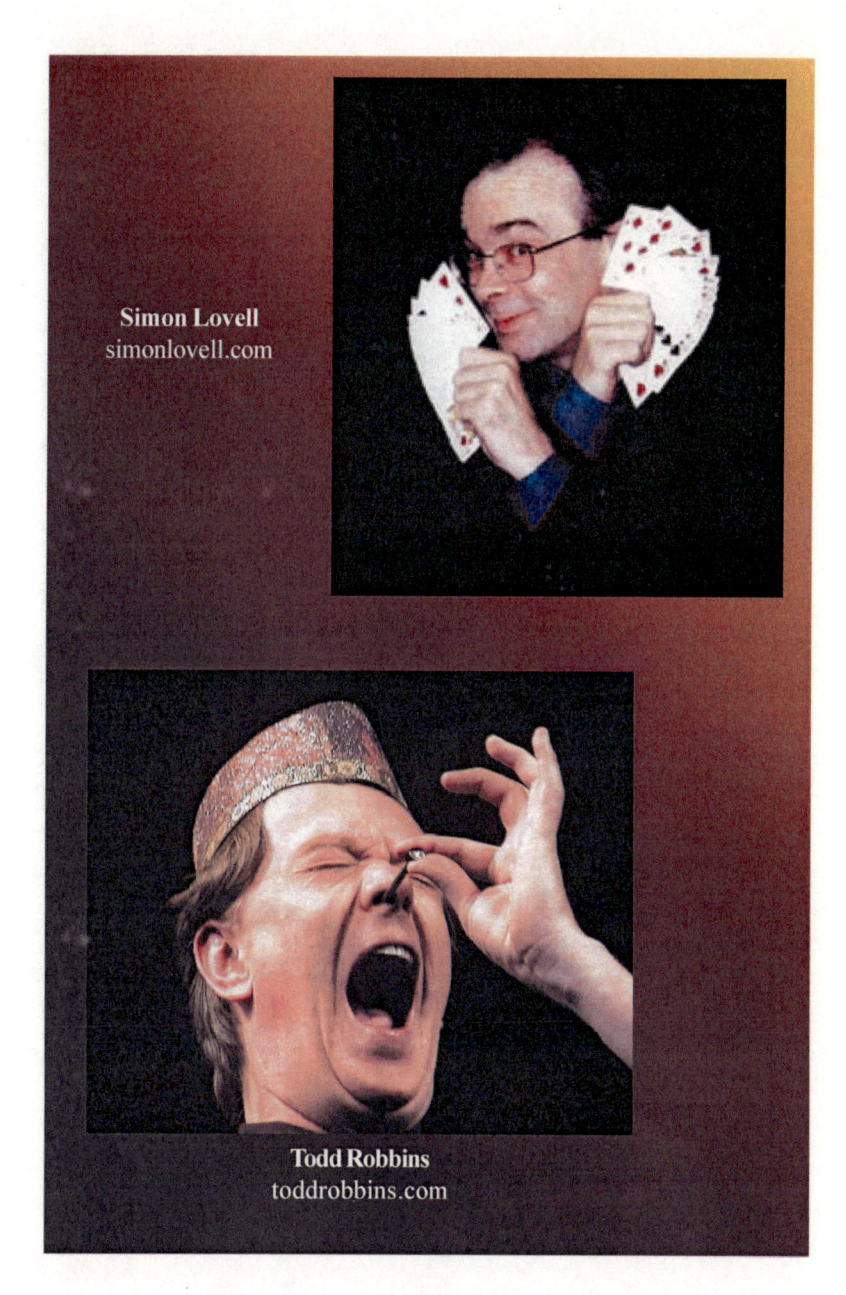

Simon Lovell
simonlovell.com

Todd Robbins
toddrobbins.com

163

Dick Haines

Larry Cisewski

John Graham
johnmagic.com

John Stetson
johnstetson.com

165

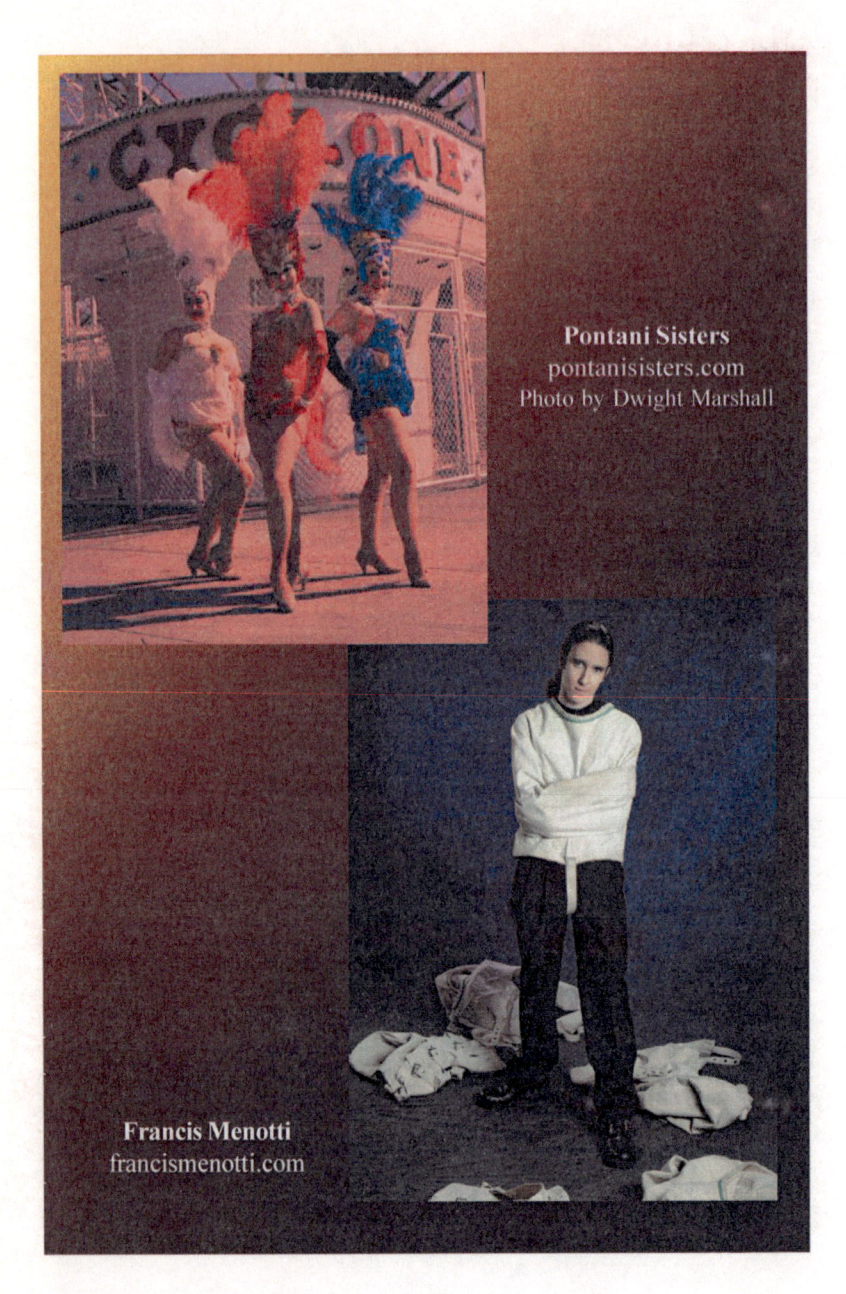

Pontani Sisters
pontanisisters.com
Photo by Dwight Marshall

Francis Menotti
francismenotti.com

Ken Pierce
(Che Che Whitecloud)

Harry & Joan Munroe
harrymknives.com

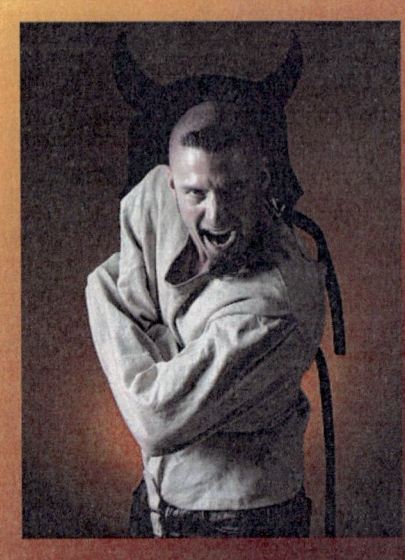

Tyler Fyre
tylerfyre.com
Photo by clycreation.com

Fred Kahl (Fredini) and Julie Atlas Muz
thisorthat.tv
Photo by Laure Leber

Ula
(The Painproof Rubber Girl)
painproofrubbergirls.com
Photo by Dan Howell

Joe Torraca
The man who introduced Throwdini
to knife throwing

A TREATISE ON THE ART AND SCIENCE OF THROWING KNIVES

by Dr. David Adamovich
THE GREAT THROWDINI

Photo by clycreation.com

A TREATISE ON THE ART AND SCIENCE OF THROWING KNIVES

THE GREAT THROWDINI — World's Fastest Knife Thrower
(David R. Adamovich, Ed.D., F.A.C.S.M.)
World Champion Knife Thrower / Professional Impalement Artist
Inductee, International Knife Throwers Hall of Fame
(516) 546-1425
876 Guy Lombardo Avenue   Freeport, New York 11520
E-mail: throwdini@knifethrower.com
www.knifethrower.com

About the Author

As a professional knife thrower and former competitive thrower Dr. David Adamovich holds world championship titles in both the IKTA and WFKT organizations and currently devotes his time to performing the impalement arts on both stage and TV. When not throwing knives he is an ordained Minister of the Gospel, has been a professor of sports sciences, is a Fellow of the American College of Sports Medicine and has published and presented over 50 articles in the areas of pocket billiards, strength training, electrocardiography, and the scientific and medical aspects of cardiovascular performance.

DISCLAIMER

Throwing knives, hawks or axes have inherent risks and must be treated as weapons with the potential to cause serious physical harm. The utmost caution must be exercised at all times to not only protect the thrower but any bystanders as well. The reader or this article assumes all responsibility for his/her actions and agrees to hold the author harmless for any untoward events that may occur. If the reader does not agree with this statement then he/she should not attempt throwing knives.

Introduction

So what's that thump sound you hear coming from your neighbor's place? You've thought he was strange, but now you've got the evidence you've always needed. What's he up to? Could he be a "closet" knife thrower? Alas, you're onto him; the Jig is Up! Just what kind of knife thrower is he? Let's now explore the most common possibilities.

Figure 1. Competition Throwing

There are three kinds of knife throwers: recreational, competition and impalement artists. (A fourth type of thrower, the martial artist, is not included within this discussion; their knives, objective and style of throwing are entirely different than discussed herein.) The recreational thrower's objective is to make the thrown knife stick, anywhere/anyhow. Their targets may be to the side of a barn, a tree, a homemade backboard, or whatever. For the most part horizontal and vertical placements are irrelevant. The competition thrower's objective is to make the thrown knife stick; not only within a specific zone or target area but a specific "bulls-eye" as well. Horizontal and vertical placements are critical in every throw. (See Figure 1)

The impalement artist's objective is to miss his "target" — human, of course; while encircling her in a manner that appears dangerously close but is safely within the thrower's margin of error.

Horizontal placement is, for the most part, relatively insignificant given a range of perhaps +/- 6" up or down. Vertical placement, on the other hand, is so critical that his "target's" life depends on it! (See Figure 2)

The number of throwers in each category diminishes significantly as you go from recreational to competition to impalement artists.

Knives

There is little disagreement as to what most knife throwers consider the minimum and maximum "ideal" throwing knife, i.e., twelve to sixteen inches in length, one to three inches in breadth, 2/16-3/16 inches thick, and weighing approximately 85 ounce/inch. Thus, a fourteen inch knife will weigh approximately twelve ounces. Despite personal preferences most recreational throwers will throw anything that sticks. Most competition throwers will throw knives around fourteen inches in length whereas most impalement artists will throw knives between fourteen and sixteen inches in length. Throwing knives less than twelve inches and more than sixteen inches in length, however, are either too light or too heavy and unwieldy, respectively. Specifically, knives less than twelve inches in length tend to lack

Figure 2. Impalement Arts

sufficient weight to penetrate their target, flop in flight rather than spin uniformly and in the words of many competition throwers, "Just don't feel right." Knives greater than sixteen inches in length are often unwieldy and a bit too "heavy" to throw comfortably. Once again, individual preferences based on what an individual first learned to throw have significant influences on what feels best and ultimately becomes one's favorite throwing knife.

Throwing knives usually have two "cutting" edges. Some have only one. (See Figure 3) It is a popular misconception to think that a throwing knife is balanced. In fact, after careful consideration most knife throwers will agree that slightly heavier toward either the blade or handle end will aid either handle or blade throws, respectively. For example, a knife with perhaps sixty percent of its weight (when measured from the center) toward the blade end will throw easier with a smoother release when thrown from the handle than when thrown from the blade. Likewise the same is true for a blade thrower being slightly heavier at the handle end. It would appear that an advantage is gained when the heavier end of the knife is that part being "whipped" while the lighter half or end is held in the hand. This observation is purely empirical but held by many experienced throwers. Moreover, a thrown object that is top heavy tends to "stick itself" and requires less effort by the thrower — tomahawks and axes to wit! OK, prove this "misbalance" concept to yourself. Hold a hammer by the handle and flip it upward to make one complete revolution so as to catch it by the handle. Easy, huh. Now attempt the same while holding the hammer by its head. Oops! Definitely not so easy as the head tends to remain away from your hand rather than fall back into it. The moral of this story…things tend to rotate nicely around their heavy end and poorly around their light end. This is another reason why knife throwers who take up tomahawk or axe throwing afterward say that hawks and axes throw and stick "easier" than knives. No wonder why!

Most target competition knives are handleless. Some throwers, on the other hand, prefer handled knives. Handle material is usually leather, hard plastic or composite material. Wrapping common electrical or duct tape around the lower third of the knife can simulate the look of a handle without adding width. Impalement artists, in particular, prefer to throw handleless knives, as there is less chance of deflection, should knife to knife contact occur. The cutting edge(s) are generally blunt and rarely sharp enough to cut your hand. Whereas these blunted edges allow the knife to be thrown from the blade, appropriate caution must still be exercised. It is advisable to keep a metal file handy to smooth out any burrs that occur when knives collide. Burrs or nicks in the metal will tear skin as your hand slides off the knife during release. Bet on it!

Stance

There are several different ways to stand when throwing a knife. Three methods prevail: planting your feet, taking one step, or running into the throw. Most throwers plant their feet and shift their weight from the back to the forward leg/foot. (See Figure 4)

Taking either one step or multiple steps results in the same terminal position, i.e., shifting your body weight toward the direction of the throw. As for the actual throwing motion most throwers will

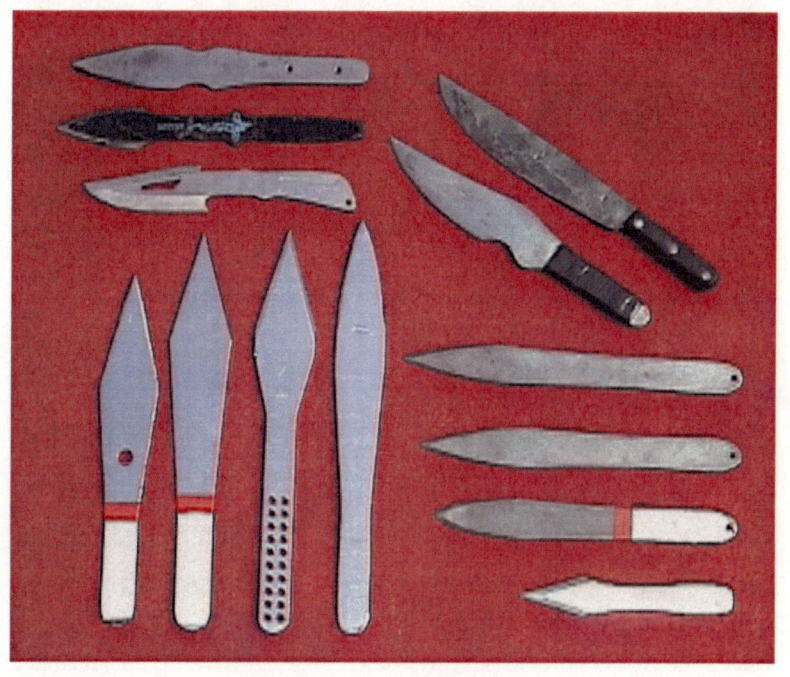

Figure 3. Throwing Knives

simulate the throw of a baseball pitcher, that is, opposite foot forward (right handed throw, left foot forward). A minority of throwers will simulate the throw of a dart thrower, that is to put the same foot forward (right-handed throw, right foot forward).

Speed of Throw (velocity from hand to target)

A thrown knife tumbles through the air handle over tip like a pinwheel between 25 and 30 mph as it leaves the throwers hand and moves toward the target. One full spin from the handle will reach the target in just under 0.3 seconds. Just how much weight shift, forward lean and waist bending a thrower puts in will help determine the speed of throw. This is easy to visualize. Consider the final upright posture and minimal body motion of a dart thrower in contrast to the forward lean of a baseball pitcher whose rear leg is off the ground and in the air as he literally falls forward at the end of his pitch. Based on this, the slower throws result from those simulating a dart throw and the faster throws are from those simulating a baseball throw.

FREQUENCY OF THROW
(RATE OF DISCHARGE FROM HAND)

The frequency (or rate) of throw is the speed at which a thrower can unload a handful of knives. It is measured as the number of knives thrown/time, OR its converse seconds/throw. Impalement artists, for the most part, will work on improving their rate of throw as it is often used in their stage routines. The frequency of throw will depend on the stunt being performed. Here is an example of measured frequencies: Paul LaCrosse 0.9 sec/throw, Fritz Brumbach 0.62 sec/throw, Ken Pierce (Che Che Whitecloud) 0.53 sec/throw,

Figure 4. Stance

The Great Throwdini 0.50 sec/throw — conversely that's 2 knives/second! The first three were measured while performing the Wheel of Death in which their assistant is standing on a rotating wheel of about six feet in circumference. LaCross threw to one side of his assistant only. Brumbach and Pierce threw to both sides, i.e., head up and head down at a wheel rotating just over one sec/revolution. (Throwdini's performance was undertaken to document just how fast a handful of knives could be discharged. This feat is documented at www.knifethrower.com under the FASTEST link).

Grip

There are two basic grips for throwing knives: the hammer (or handshake) grip and the thumb grip. (See Figures 5 and 6)

The latter takes on its name because the thrower places his/her thumb along the upper spine of the knife vs. along the inside as in the hammer grip. Regardless of which method is used all four fingers (index to pinky) encircle the knife in a medium to soft grip. Very few, if any, throwers hold their knife in a "death" grip in which it couldn't be pulled out of their hand. Some throwers "pinch" or hold their knives so lightly that if not careful it could slip right through their fingers when brought back prior to commencing their forward swing.

I hold the knife with three fingers only so that it's tip or handle rests in the middle of my palm for a very light, pinch grip.

Wind-up

Simply stated, a knife is thrown in a manner similar to the way in which the thrower would naturally throw a ball. Unlike a baseball pitch, however, knife throwers do not go through an elaborate wind-up prior to the actual throw and release.

Figure 5. Hammer Grip

Figure 6. Thumb Grip

Simply stated, the knife begins in front of the thrower, is swung upward and backward and is then swung/thrown forward away from the thrower and toward the target. All throwers will bring their knife at least as far back as their head directing the knife anywhere from skyward to directly rearward, 90° to 180° from the face of the target respectively. Several actually let their knife drop so far back that it points straight down toward their feet touching their back near the shoulder blade! (See Figure 7) Rapid-fire throwing, on the other hand, is performed with a short snappy throw with virtually no wind-up.

SWING/Throw & Release

Often misunderstood and the topic of much debate, confusion and argument among throwers are the rules of physics that come into play throughout a knife's flight. On the one hand, who cares so long as it sticks. On the other, it's just nice to know the facts for those who are scientifically inclined. Throughout this entire section the reader will come to the conclusion that THE THROWER'S HAND ACTUALLY SLIPS OFF THE KNIFE AS THE KNIFE PASSES THROUGH THE APEX OF ITS SWING, THAT IS, AT THE PEAK OF ITS TRAJECTORY! (See Figure 4) The subsequent rotation of the knife, i.e., its spinning about the center like a pinwheel is a result of the free-end rotating faster than the held-end at the moment of release.

A thrown knife is acted upon by several forces throughout its journey: centripetal (center-seeking) – the force exerted by the arm and hand in holding throughout its circular path prior to release (not unlike an object twirled on a string); centrifugal (center-fleeing) – the force exerted by the knife as it attempts to break away from the throwers grip, gravity – the force on the knife after it leaves the

Figure 7. Start of Throw

throwers hand (ultimately causing the knife to hit the earth if doesn't find a target first), and finally rotational – the force exerted on the knife as it rotates (tumbles/pivots) about its long axis. If this didn't happen, the knife would propel forward like a dart (horizontally) or move from point A to point B in a vertical plane; both in contrast to rotating like a pinwheel in the air.

Having said that, here's the physics of it all. Centripetal force pulls in on the knife. Centrifugal force pulls outward on the knife. The two remain balanced as the knife moves in its circular path (similar to a ball on a string) prior to release. Centrifugal force is mistakenly thought to cause the knife to "fly" out of its circular path when released by the hand. Rather, it is the removal of the centripetal force that allows the knife to travel in a straight line following its release from the hand. Following Newton's First Law (every object in a state of uniform motion tends to remain in that state of motion unless an external force is applied to it) the knife released at the apex of its trajectory will propel forward (or vertically) in a straight line toward the target. Once in flight its horizontal motion will come under the influence of gravity.

Based on the above, it is improper to evaluate the point at which a thrower "throws" the knife. In reality THE THROWER'S HAND ACTUALLY SLIPS OFF THE KNIFE AS THE KNIFE PASSES THROUGH THE APEX OF ITS SWING! At the apex of the arm swing (arm almost straight) and at the moment the hand slides off the knife, the knife flies **tangentially** forward in a straight line toward the target, spinning and at the same time falling under the influence of gravity. Release too soon, the knife flies skyward. Release too late, the knife flies earthward. Release too late and you impale your foot!

NUMBER OF SPINS

What is referred to as one "full" spin, i.e., held by the handle and thrown for one complete revolution is actually one and one quarter spins! For example, consider the blade held for a one half spin throw: the hand slides off the blade when the handle is pointed skyward (90° perpendicular to the face of the target). (See Figure 8)

It makes one quarter spin so the handle is now aimed at the target. It then spins an additional 180°, or one half revolution, to penetrate the target point first. Thus, each particular throw — the half, the one, the one and one half, etc. are actually spinning an additional 90° from the point of release through its final position, sticking **point first** at the face of the target.

Figure 8. Hand Sliding Off Knife

With regard to the knife spinning or tumbling handle over tip consider the following. The knife is held at either end, blade or handle — not in the middle like a baton. (In contrast, the baton is made to spin like a pinwheel as its thrower rapidly rotates the wrist similar to turning a faucet on/off). As the knife leaves the hand it has no choice but to spin/rotate like a pinwheel in the same manner a broom handle falls end over end when toppling off the palm of your hand. It is virtually impossible to throw the knife "flat" toward the target without it spinning end over end. The only way to accomplish this would be to "push" or "slide" the knife forward, similar to a martial arts type of release, rather than discussed herein.

Follow-through

One can reasonably argue that once the knife leaves the hand it doesn't matter what you do with your arm. Well, yes and no. Two things are of paramount importance in letting go of and in following-through after releasing the knife: 1) do not twist or snap your wrist, and 2) initially following downward vs. across the body with your forearm. Twisting the wrist (faucet on/off) will cause the knife to hit the target horizontally versus vertically, resulting in a dropped knife. Presuming you are throwing an overhand vs. sidearm throw (as seen by some baseball pitchers) your arm should continue on its circular path, forward and downward after release. (See Figure 9) Snapping the wrist (like a volleyball spike) is discussed further down.

Throwing your arm across your body, i.e., so that your hand ends on the opposite side could have a negative influence on the outcome of your throw. Such motion will cause the thrown knife to stick in a line between 1 o'clock and 7 o'clock across the face of the target; thus reducing left to right vertical alignment. Bringing your arm straight downward after release will force you to swing your arm from behind,

Figure 9. Arm Continues Downward

straight toward the target, and then downward in a circular motion that is vertically aligned with the target; insuring consistent vertical alignment in all throws. Remember that for both competition and impalement arts (especially in the impalement arts) a knife thrown too far left or right will either miss the bulls-eye or impale the human "target" — neither of these choices is acceptable, particularly the latter! Horizontal placement is determined by where within the circular path of the arm the knife is allowed to slip from the hand. Allowing for gravity the knife must be released at precisely the correct point to propel forward, tumble and ultimately stick where intended — neither too high nor too low.

In summary, the DELIVERY swing begins from behind the body. As the knife is brought overhead and forward the elbow is starting to align itself with the target. When the elbow points directly at the target (the upper arm or humerus aligns horizontally to the ground), the elbow stops moving as the forearm acts like a catapult, releasing the knife just prior to the forearm being horizontal to the ground. Finally the entire arm follows through, initially downward vs. across the body toward the opposite hip. (See Figure 10)

Targets

The right target is anything (inanimate, of course) the knife sticks into and isn't going to cost you a lot of money to replace. Doors and walls are not ideal targets. For starters the easiest, largest and safest target to make is by using a twelve foot length piece of 2 x 12 commercially available lumber. Several choices are Douglas fir, Universal lumbar, pine or cedar, from cheapest to most expensive. The secret to a good target is SOFT wood. (The ultimate piece of mush that acts like a sponge when wet is palm. A fresh round of palm watered down prior to throwing can literally swallow a twelve inch knife six inches deep or even accept a knife that hits vertically, sticking the entire length of the knife from handle to blade). Cut the twelve foot piece of lumbar in half, use a couple of cross-sticks to join the two six foot pieces together across their backside. You now have a target that is six feet tall by two feet wide.

For beginners learning to throw either a half spin (holding the blade end of the knife) or a full spin (from the handle) a target this broad and tall in nearly impossible to miss. It is further advisable to put either a piece of carpet, folded cardboard or rubber matting on the

Figure 10. Incorect - Across Body towards the opposite hip or knee

floor that extends at least three feet from the target. Beginner knife throwers tend to pick up more "bounced" knives than remove "stuck" knives from their targets. Rubber or carpet matting will save both the floor and knives from considerable damage. From here the thrower can progress to hanging tree rounds in front of the previously mentioned backboard/target. The most common tree round is pine or other soft wood cut into eight inch thick discs between fourteen and sixteen inches across. An eight inch target ring with a two and one half inch bulls-eye painted on both sides of the round is an ideal target to begin with. When one side becomes worn you simply spin the target around and begin chewing up the other side. Such targets can withstand thousands of sticks before being discarded. An insider's trick is to either soak the target in water or hose it down prior to throwing. This softens the wood, allows for fewer bounces and slows down the chipping and splitting that occurs with dry wood.

Distance vs. Spin

Depending on arm length and knife length there is a reasonable distance to begin experimenting within. All one half spins are thrown from the blade end. All full spins are thrown from the handle end. The generally accepted tournament spins and distances are: one half spin from eight feet, one full spin from twelve feet, one and one half spin from fifteen feet, two full spins from eighteen feet, and two and one half spins from twenty one feet.

Usually success will be found within one foot forward or backward of those lines. THE IDEAL STICK IS HORIZONTAL TO THE GROUND. The rule to follow in determining whether you are too close or too far from the target is, "handle up — move up." Likewise, move back if the handle is down. (See Figure 11) The distance to change is about one half the length of your shoe. In a handle up profile the knife had too much time (or distance) to turn, thus having **over** rotated. In the handle down profile there wasn't enough time (or distance) to turn and the knife hasn't gone through a full rotation, thus having **under** rotated. To accommodate for non-horizontal sticks change your distance by no more than six inches at a time and see what happens. When several sticks occur in a row

Figure 11. Perfect & Handle Down

that are either up, straight or down will you have determined where you should stand.

If your distance from the target hasn't changed and your throws are sticking in all three positions it is because you are not throwing consistently or you are moving your hand either up or down on the handle. Generally speaking, if you move your hand toward the center of the knife by even one inch you will cause the knife to tumble or spin at a slower rate. This will have the same effect as moving further from the target by as much as one foot. On the other hand, a trick used to force the knife to spin faster (as commonly used by impalement artists to "cheat" the distance) is to "pull the trigger" as you slide your hand off the knife. Pulling back with your hand just slightly on the knife imparts an additional amount of spin, thus enabling the thrower to stand closer than what the "normal" distance would be.

Wrist Snapping (DON'T)

The technique of "pulling the trigger" is not to be confused with "snapping" the wrist — an absolute no-no in knife throwing. To understand the difference between the two imagine the motion used spiking a volleyball downward over the net in which you flex your wrist when hitting the ball. This is not done in knife throwing. Snapping the wrist has the effect of over rotating the knife, prematurely terminating your follow-through and causing the knife to spin earthward rather than forward. It's easy to do and difficult to stop once it becomes habit. One technique to avoid this from the beginning is to have someone quickly pull a knife from your hand as you slowly release your grip on the handle. Listen carefully to the sound the knife makes as it slides from your hand. Attempt to simulate that sound when throwing the knife and you will be doing it properly. Suddenly opening your hand in contrast to easing the tension of your grip, thus sliding your hand downward and away from the knife, is incorrect and causes an abnormal, uncomfortable release.

The Great Throwdini

Photo by markmurraystudio.com